Library Science Text Series

Nonprint Cataloging
for
Multimedia Collections

Nonprint Cataloging for Multimedia Collections

A Guide Based on AACR 2

By
JoAnn V. Rogers

1982
Libraries Unlimited, Inc. • *Littleton, Colorado*

LIBRARIES UNLIMITED, INC.
P.O. Box 263
Littleton, Colorado 80160

Library of Congress Cataloging in Publication Data

Rogers, JoAnn V., 1940-
   Nonprint cataloging for multimedia collections.

   Includes bibliographies and index.
   1. Cataloging of non-book materials--Handbooks,
manuals, etc. 2. Descriptive cataloging--Rules--
Handbooks, manuals, etc. I. Anglo-American
cataloguing rules. II. Title.
Z695.66.R63 1982   025.3'47   82-8986
ISBN 0-87287-284-X

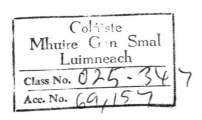
Libraries Unlimited books are bound with Type II nonwoven material that meets
and exceeds National Association of State Textbook Administrators' Type II
nonwoven material specifications Class A through E.

Preface

The information in this book, based on my research on bibliographic control of nonprint materials and current library practices in the application of the *Anglo-American Cataloguing Rules*, 2nd ed. (Chicago: American Library Association, 1978), is intended for catalogers and those responsible for determining cataloging policies in library agencies. The introductory chapter focuses on factors which affect nonprint collections in various types of libraries and discusses bibliographic control of nonprint materials. Chapter II discusses selected rules presented in the *AACR 2* Introduction and in Chapter I, which cover the rules generally applicable to all formats, both print and nonprint. Although the rules in the *AACR 2* chapters pertaining to nonprint take precedence over those in the General Rules (1.0) where there is a difference between the specific rules for nonprint and the general rules, many of the general rules are needed for description. Those most commonly used for nonprint are selected for explanation in this text. Chapters III through VIII provide discussion, interpretation, and illustrative examples of selected rules from Chapters 3, 6, 7, 8, 10, and 11 of *AACR 2*. Those rules which are most often used or pose the most problems for catalogers are selected for discussion. Included at the end of each of these chapters are examples of bibliographic description of individual nonprint items covered by the rules in the chapter. Examples are representative of the types of nonprint items found in many integrated, multimedia collections. This limited number of examples cannot possibly deal with the infinite number of challenges which the cataloger will encounter. These are intended to provide examples based on the discussion in the book, and not to serve as a template for cataloging. The bibliographic facts of an item in hand seldom match those of any other example. No manual of examples can substitute for a good understanding of the intent and directions for presenting bibliographic information provided in the rules.

Chapter IX presents a brief discussion of rules of particular importance to nonprint materials in *AACR 2*, Chapter 21, "Choice of Access Points." Some discussion is related to choice of main entry and other is concerned with added entries. *AACR 2* allows a great deal of flexibility in choice of access points. Each library needs to consider the rules and set library policy concerning choice and number of added entries. A number of catalog examples at the end of Chapters III through VIII include some suggested added entries. These are not prescriptive and are not intended to include all of the desirable or possible added entries for any cataloging record. Only those which might be overlooked by the cataloger are given on some examples.

Organized according to the structure of the rules in *AACR 2*, this book gives information and makes suggestions to aid the cataloger in making judgments and decisions necessary in the process of developing a bibliographic description for nonprint materials. Levels of description, various alternative methods for presenting descriptive information, and optional additions of information to the basic descriptions are discussed and illustrated. The physical characteristics of media (nonprint) formats are explained to aid the cataloger in recording the physical description of the materials in the collection.

Sources of additional information are listed in the appendices at the end of the text. The first bibliography (Appendix I) lists cataloging aids which include sources of catalog copy, cataloging formats used by bibliographic utilities, and sources for policy decisions of major libraries related to rule application and interpretation. Selected titles which explain in detail the physical characteristics of nonprint formats are listed in the second bibliography. A bibliography of bibliographies (Appendix III) provides a list of titles which supply bibliographic information for many published nonprint materials. A sample of the types of bibliographies which provide useful information for the cataloger is included in a listing of selected, general bibliographies and directories (Appendix V). These can provide information needed for bibliographic description of nonprint materials. Access to all of these types of reference sources can enhance the cataloger's ability to provide complete and accurate bibliographic description of materials.

Techniques which have been used by librarians to provide bibliographic access to nonprint materials are numerous and varied. Factors which have influenced cataloging practices include the types and numbers of items which a library collects, organization of the materials in an omnimedia collection or in a number of special collections, the ability of catalogers to deal with nonprint formats, and the state of the art of available cataloging rules and manuals. Prior to the publication of *AACR 2*, many different guides, manuals, and books of rules for cataloging and processing nonprint vied for adoption in libraries. The rules provided in the first edition of the Anglo-American code, even with revised chapters for nonprint, were considered inadequate or inappropriate by many catalogers of nonprint. Lacking a national standard which was universally accepted, librarians either struggled with *AACR 1* or adopted practices touted by one of the other guides or manuals. None of the cataloging aids, prior to *AACR 2*, applied a standard bibliographic descriptive format to nonprint, and few of these aids consistently applied accepted bibliographic principles in the formulation of the rules which they presented. Many of the cataloging aids did not even provide an adequate body of rules, but instead, presented examples from which the cataloger had to infer the rules.

For a number of years, many librarians have been painfully aware of the problems associated with cataloging nonprint. Until 1978, however, no single system or code was significantly superior to any other. The methods for cataloging nonprint presented in *AACR 2* represent some significant changes and improvements over previously available cataloging aids. Most significant is the application of the international standard bibliographic description (ISBD) for both print and nonprint which enables the records to be used in manual and automated catalogs. Other improvements include expanded coverage of the number and types of formats, consistent application of basic principles for all formats, consistent application of general rules when possible, and standardization of terms related to the definition of nonprint formats.

Because of these developments, which make it possible to provide better bibliographic control of nonprint, many library agencies will want to consider adoption of *AACR 2*. Librarians should evaluate their current practices, learn about the coverage of nonprint in *AACR 2*, and compare the quality of the bibliographic records of the two systems. The needs of the library users should also be studied and considered before the adoption of a new code.

In defining the user population, librarians must keep in mind the current and future impact of library networking and resource sharing. Single-type and multi-type library networks, sharing bibliographic records and materials in all formats, will be the pattern of library development for the future. A standard bibliographic description based on consistently applied rules and developed from sound principles is the cornerstone to bibliographic networking. Few libraries will be able to justify practices which separate them from this mainstream. Most users will benefit from this standardization and expansion of rules covering nonprint. It will result in standardization of the catalog record and the improved quality of the cataloging itself.

If the code is adopted, other choices remain to be made. These choices include policy decisions about the three levels of bibliographic description allowed in the rules, alternate methods for recording information about formats, and addition of optional elements of information. These choices allow some flexibility on the local level while maintaining the standard framework within which all materials are described.

The first two chapters of this text identify and consider some of the facts and issues related to bibliographic control of nonprint materials. Chapter II provides an overview of nonprint in *AACR 2*. Librarians considering adopting the code and librarians planning to actually adopt the code will find this background information useful in the decision-making process. The remaining chapters deal with the rules for cataloging media formats and are intended for catalogers working with the code in applying the rules to media materials. The information will supplement the *AACR 2* text by discussing and illustrating selected rules of particular importance to the formats and to the library.

As evidenced by the interpretations and modifications found necessary by the Library of Congress (LC) in working with the new code, all cataloging problems and challenges are not definitively and finally addressed in this second edition of the rules. This first attempt at a real integration of the rules for nonprint with those for print may be only a beginning. Undoubtedly, the rules for nonprint will evolve as catalogers and nonprint specialists work with the materials and the rules. In some places, clarification is needed, expansion of the rules would answer some unanswered questions, and some changes may be necessary.

It should be remembered that *AACR 2* is intended for general, multimedia libraries of all sizes, but in its present form, it may not be sufficient for archival or large special collections of nonprint materials. As this book goes to press, the preliminary draft of "Rules for Cataloging Graphic Materials" prepared by the Prints and Photographs Division of the Library of Congress is being circulated for comments from concerned librarians. Another manual for archival film collections is planned. Hopefully, these will be compatible with *AACR 2* and international standard bibliographic description. If they are not, the promise which *AACR 2* holds for increased integration of print and nonprint bibliographic records will be only partly realized. Special collections may remain outside the mainstream, and catalogers will have to choose camps. This would be unfortunate indeed. This book is based on the rules as given and includes comments about practice and policy announced by the Descriptive Cataloging Division of the Library of Congress. No attempt has been made to suggest modifications, although problem areas are identified and discussed.

The large number of nonprint formats and the different types of intellectual and artistic content contained in each of the formats present a multifaceted challenge to the cataloger of nonprint materials. The coverage of nonprint in *AACR 2*, greatly expanded and more detailed than the rules for nonprint in *AACR 1*, reflects the acknowledgment of the profession that the task is a complex one which deserves in-depth treatment in the rules. Although some problems still exist, *AACR 2* is the best tool available to help in providing bibliographic control of nonprint material in library collections. Once catalogers learn to apply the rules to media materials, the advantages of the amount of detail which they contain will become evident. Directions are given for recording almost all of the bibliographic facts of nonprint formats. Less creative improvization is needed than with any previous code. Catalog records for nonprint materials using *AACR 2* will be more uniform than has been possible in the past, print and nonprint catalogs can be more easily integrated, and users can now expect catalog records to contain the standard elements of description for both print and nonprint. The change is a major one which should further the development of libraries as multimedia institutions.

For their assistance in preparing this book, I want to thank several people who gave generously of their time and talent: Barbara Van Nostrand, who with great skill and dedication accomplished the difficult task of typing the first draft and revision; Carolyn Havens, who helped in supplying examples; Robin Nelson and Robin Wagner, student assistants, and Linda Newman, who proofread the first draft.

For the professional dedication which motivated Dr. Doris H. Clack to make valuable suggestions and corrections in the edited copy, I am particularly grateful.

I also want to express my appreciation to the University of Kentucky for allowing me sabbatical leave to use the fruits of my research on bibliographic control of nonprint to prepare these guidelines. I hope that the information in the book will serve as an explanation of the present state of the art in cataloging nonprint media materials and will help catalogers with the challenging task of preparing bibliographic descriptions for these materials.

Table of Contents

List of Figures

I

Bibliographic Control of Nonprint

In order to appreciate the role of the Anglo-American cataloging code or any other system used for describing and accessing nonprint materials, several basic issues related to bibliographic control of nonprint materials should be considered. The purpose of adopting and applying a cataloging code for print and nonprint media in a library or media center is to provide effective bibliographic control of the collection for its users. Adequate bibliographic control of nonprint materials is a challenge to the library and media professions for several reasons. These reasons are related to:

- the nature of the materials
- the diverse nature of existing collections
- the needs of users of nonprint materials
- cataloging practices prior to *AACR 2* used for bibliographic control.

NONPRINT MEDIA MATERIALS

The first challenge for librarians and media specialists working with nonprint formats is to gain an understanding of the physical characteristics and the content, both intellectual and artistic, of the many different types of materials found in nonprint library collections. To facilitate bibliographic description, nonprint materials are defined according to their physical characteristics and are grouped according to common characteristics. A problem basic to bibliographic control of nonprint has been the lack of standardization of terms related to the materials. This is partly the result of the dynamic nature of the media industry itself. The characteristics of the formats are constantly changing as technological advances have made possible evolutionary and some revolutionary changes in the materials. Also, librarians, users of nonprint, and those associated with the creation, production, publication, and dissemination of nonprint formats view the materials from significantly different perspectives in terms of both the medium and the message.

A large proportion of commercially produced, nonprint materials are collected by educational institutions. Recognizing the need for definition of terms and a system of categorization of nonprint materials, the National Center for Educational Statistics has published a handbook to

> provide a classified structure of concepts, terminology, definitions, and suggested units of measure in order to better serve modern educational information systems, to assist in planning and decision making, and to help ensure compatible and comparable recording and reporting of educational technology data.[1]

Their classification of terms, defined in another section of the handbook, is as follows:

TERM

MATERIALS
  Recorded Materials
   Audiorecording
    Audiocard, Recorded
    Audiodisc
    Audiotape, Recorded
     Audiotape Reel, Recorded
     Audiotape Cassette, Recorded
     Audiotape Cartridge, Recorded
     Other Recorded Audiotapes
    Audiopage, Recorded
    Dictation/Transcription Belt, Recorded
    Talking Book
    Other Audiorecordings
  Computer Materials
   Computer Card, Punched
   Computer Printout
   Computer Program
   Computer-Magnetic Tape, Recorded
   Other Recorded Computer Materials
  Electronic Display Materials
   Videotape, Recorded
    Videotape Reel, Recorded
    Videotape Cassette, Recorded
    Videotape Cartridge, Recorded
    Other Recorded Videotape
   Videodisc, Recorded
   Other Recorded Electronic Display Materials
  Projected and Magnified Materials
   Aperture Card
   Microform
    Microfiche
    Microfilm Reel
    Micro-opaque
    Ultrafiche
    Other Microform Materials
   Microscope Slide
   Filmstrip
    Filmstrip, Silent
    Filmstrip, Sound
    Other Filmstrips
   Slide
   Slide/Audiotape
   Audioslide
   Overhead Transparency

Stereograph
Hologram
Motion Picture
Motion Picture, 16mm.
Motion Picture, 8mm.
Motion Picture, Super 8mm.
Other Motion Pictures
Other Projected and Magnified Materials
Printed/Pictorial Materials
Book
Chart
Map
Picture
Art Print
Study Print
Photograph
Other Pictures
Serial
Periodical
Other Serials
Other Printed/Pictorial Materials
Three-Dimensional Materials
Diorama
Exhibit
Game
Globe
Mock-up
Model
Realia
Simulation Material
Educational Toy
Other Three-Dimensional Materials
Kit
Multimedia Kit
Learning Package
Other Kits
Other Recorded Materials[2]

The title of the handbook *A Handbook of Standard Terminology and a Guide for Recording and Reporting Information about Educational Technology*, illustrates one perspective on nonprint materials, that of the educator. Nonprint formats are viewed as tools of education. Other terms commonly applied by educators are "instructional materials" or "instructional resources," "audiovisual aids," "audiovisual media," or "audiovisual materials." Some of the terms included in this list such as "learning package" and "simulation material" are not descriptive of the physical characteristics of the materials but are related to their intended educational use.

If the definition of terms used in a bibliographic system is to be appropriate for all types of materials in different library settings, the definitions should relate to the physical characteristics of the materials themselves. Even when attempting to define terms with this guideline, differences exist in the terms applied to these materials by librarians, users, creators, manufacturers, and media specialists. When trying to achieve a standardization of generic terms and common categories across international boundaries, another dimension is added to the problem. *AACR 2* has addressed these problems by offering definitions for the basic terms and by organizing the formats into categories sharing common physical characteristics.

Some differences in terminology have not been resolved, resulting in two different lists of terms used for material designation. The use of standard terms for North American libraries will insure, however, that terms will be consistently applied in all types of libraries in this country. Differences are relatively minor, and the categories reflected in the organization of the rules into chapters for different categories of media are the same in this country and elsewhere. The definition of terms in *AACR 2* is discussed in greater detail in Chapter II of this text in the sections dealing with "General Material Designation" and specific medium designators.

In addition to standardizing terms used to describe generic format types, *AACR 2* has standardized the location in the bibliographic record for information about the physical characteristics of the formats and has specified the necessary elements of description related to specific types of formats. This is a great step forward in providing adequate bibliographic information related to the nature of the materials.

Besides dealing with the complex nature and number of types of nonprint formats being commercially published and locally produced, any system for bibliographic description and control of nonprint also must allow for the diverse nature of creation, publication, and dissemination of nonprint. Information about all of these activities and the associated individuals and groups related to the production of nonprint materials is necessary for bibliographic description.

MEDIA INDUSTRY

Unlike the book publishing industry, the media industry is a rather amorphous one. It consists of thousands of different companies and individuals, some of which produce only several items in perhaps only one format. Others produce hundreds of items yearly, in different formats, with different types of content. One media publisher, such as Encyclopaedia Britannica Educational Corporation, may produce educational media on all grade levels, in many subject areas, and in a variety of formats—16mm film, 8mm film, 8mm single-concept film loops, filmstrips with and without sound, discs, cassettes, overhead transparencies, study prints, multimedia kits, slides, and programmed learning packages. Another media publisher, such as the publication operation of the Nelson Gallery of the Atkins Museum in Kansas City, may publish only 2x2-inch slides of art objects in the gallery. These organizations represent two extremes. There are many others which fall somewhere between these two.

Unlike the book publishing industry, the media industry is not dominated by a relatively few, large publishing enterprises, although there are some companies which do a large volume of nonprint business. *Audiovisual Market Place*, an annual list of organizations, firms, activities, and personnel, in its 1979 volume lists 1,300 producers which they define as firms which are active in production, for their own account. Distributors, those who distribute material created by others, and production companies, those firms which produce material under contract to others, are listed separately. They are not part of the 1,300 "publishers." The listing of producers and distributors published by the National Information Center for Educational Media (NICEM) contains over 8,000 names in its 1975 *Index to Producers and Distributors.* The NICEM 1978 Update lists about 1,200 additional names. Each entry indicates the type of activities in which the company engages. Some of the companies listed are only distributors. The listing of publishers in *Audiovisual Market Place* includes information about yearly publishing output, when it is supplied by the producers, as well as information about the formats, subject areas, and audience levels of materials which the organization produces. From this information, the audiovisual buyer can determine which companies are major producers and which ones are more limited and specialized. Output varies greatly and is not consistent from year to year. Some companies produce only a handful of items, while others regularly produce several hundred items in various formats.

The media industry is a very dynamic and flexible one, often responding to current demand in the marketplace for nonprint materials, produced in particular formats, for specific purposes. This is true of both large commercial companies and of smaller companies and individuals.

In addition to large commercial companies, there are many types of organizations and some individuals who publish nonprint formats. These include free-lance, producer-publishers; corporations which publish materials to promote their products or industry; non-profit organizations with public information objectives; tax supported governmental agencies producing material for the public and the specialist; and educational institutions, from the elementary through professional and technical programs, which package and sell anything from a single slide to an entire mediated, college-level course. Any person or organization offering nonprint media for sale or for free distribution can be considered a publisher of nonprint material. Any code for bibliographic description of nonprint must accommodate factual information about the publication of nonprint materials emanating from all of the various sources.

LOCALLY PRODUCED MATERIALS

Libraries also find themselves to be the collectors and distributors of nonprint materials which are not for sale in multiple copies but have been produced to answer a specific need, usually in an educational setting. Materials which are produced by the talent and staff associated with a school which is to house the materials are usually known as local production materials. Some "locally produced materials" may be planned and designed by local individuals but then farmed out to a production company, which can be located anywhere. The fact that the material is available in very limited quantities and has not been formally or commercially published determines its status as a "local production." Some nonprint items originate as local productions and, if their usefulness is not limited to one setting, move into the area of regularly published material with limited availability. Some material produced for educational purposes by medical schools, for example, is originally conceived and produced for one institution, but may be made available in multiple copies to other institutions which have similar needs. The medical library network, through its project AVLINE, is attempting to identify materials in this category which, although locally produced, may meet common needs in medical education. In order to be included in the AVLINE computerized information bank, the materials must be recommended and must be available nationally for loan or for purchase.

As techniques for production and duplication of nonprint materials become less complicated and less expensive in terms of necessary equipment and technical know-how, libraries are finding their nonprint collections growing with locally produced materials. Slides, slide-tape programs, audiotape, videotape, transparencies, and multimedia kits are being produced locally in increasing numbers. As libraries evolve into multimedia institutions, many of these materials, which once were not collected by libraries, are playing a larger role in their collection development and services.

For many years, teachers in elementary and secondary schools have been planning and producing educational materials in nonprint formats. Certification requirements in most states include course work in the preparation of educational materials. The 1975 standards for school media centers, *Media Programs: District and School*, include some guiding principles which state:

1) Production is performed at both the district and building level.
2) The production program includes the possibility for design and creation of materials by students, teachers, and media staff.[3]

The school district production program is planned to extend the school building level program. It is suggested that building level programs include the following capabilities:

Graphics: preparation of visuals, including dry mounting, laminating, and transparencies

Photography: black and white photography, color slides, silent 8mm film

Television and radio: videotape recording

Audiotape: recording and duplication of sound recordings.[4]

The district wide production program includes:

Graphics: visuals for curriculum use and also for public information, staff development, and administrative presentations

Photography: still photography for black and white prints and slides, motion picture photography for super 8mm and 16mm which may be done by contract with a production company

Television and radio: produces instructional television and radio or contracts with other agencies for production, receives and records educational radio and video broadcasts, collects videotapes

Audiotapes: produces and copies audiotapes and uses high speed reel-to-reel and cassette duplicators

Kits, models, and displays: designs and produces kits, models and other learning packages.[5]

Clearly, if schools attempt to follow many of the guidelines set forth in these standards, the school media center will be producing many materials which should be acquired and housed in the school media center or library.

Post secondary educational programs including vocational, technical, paraprofessional, junior or two-year college programs are also producing media materials and experiencing expanding media programs in their libraries. The media center, using materials produced by the instructional staff of junior or community colleges, business schools, and other types of training schools for purposes of individualized instruction, is adding to the number of local productions which their institutions collect. Although four-year academic programs and graduate programs, other than the health science professional preparation programs, have been the slowest to provide for local production in curriculum use, many academic institutions are catching up with the instructional potential of nonprint formats. Academic libraries are beginning to incorporate nonprint materials and services into their programs. Often, production is done by a unit separate from the library on a university campus, but much of the material produced does find its way into the library's collection.

Public libraries and special libraries are less likely to have extensive production facilities. As public libraries become more active in cable activities, however, they are making use of more media material and in some cases, have production studios and facilities. Many organizations which have their own library collections also support production of media and collect the materials which are published by the organizations. Any code used for bibliographic control of nonprint media, in any of the libraries which collect local production, must provide rules for recording information related to locally produced material, as well as that purchased from commercial organizations. *AACR 2* provides rules for these types of materials.

NONPRINT MEDIA COLLECTIONS

The numerous existing patterns of collection, bibliographic description, subject analysis, and organization of media materials in different types of libraries have evolved without the benefit of standardized methods. All types of libraries including public, school, academic, and special or research libraries, which are separate from or included in these types of libraries, collect nonprint formats and provide some type of bibliographic access to the materials. Various methods for accessing the materials have been adopted by these agencies. Some methods are based on *AACR 1*, and others are dictated by local and special needs. Omnimedia collections, those which attempt to integrate all of the nonprint formats with print materials, are most likely to attempt to apply the same systems of bibliographic control to both print and nonprint. Even if print and nonprint are not integrated in storage arrangements, omnimedia collections often attempt to integrate the bibliographic records for both nonprint and print into an omnimedia catalog. When nonprint collections are separate from print, however, bibliographic records for these separate nonprint collections are often separate from those for print in either one or several special catalogs.

The nature of the content of educational media materials and the fact that nonprint materials are used in school instruction are two good reasons for school media specialists to provide bibliographic access in an integrated, omnimedia catalog. All materials used as instructional resources should be accessed in similar ways. Many school media centers have attempted to integrate their catalogs as well as their collections. With the omnimedia approach of *AACR 2*, most schools will want to adopt the new code and apply it to all of the materials in their collections.

In schools where audiovisual services remain separate from library services, problems of adequate access to nonprint materials often exist. Some schools still have not applied the techniques of library science to collections of media (nonprint) materials and have not attempted to provide access through an omnimedia catalog. One technique used in these types of collections is to categorize the materials according to curriculum areas, which provides unifaceted access to materials which may, in fact, be used for many purposes. However, standards for school media programs emphasize the importance of a unified print and nonprint collection. Now that *AACR 2* provides a practical solution to the problems associated with integration of school media collections, even those schools with a separate media program will want to consider integration of instructional resources, at least in a unified catalog, if not also in terms of storage or service.

Media collections in public libraries are of several different types. Some small and medium sized public libraries have collected nonprint materials for the general user which are integrated with the print collection. These materials may or may not be accessed in an omnimedia catalog. If they are, and if *AACR 2* is adopted for print materials, the logical choice would be to also adopt *AACR 2* for nonprint. Public libraries, particularly large ones, however, also have large, special collections of nonprint for the special or research user. Often, these collections are not accessed in the general omnimedia catalog. Many of these collections are accessed in separate catalogs which are based on cataloging procedures somewhat different from those used for books or media materials for the general user.

The most common types of collections which contain nonprint in public libraries are those collections of special formats or those collections designed for specific types of users. Separate film collections, picture collections, slide collections, and collections of art prints are examples of format collections in public libraries. Book catalogs for film collections are common, and bibliographic records for films are seldom contained in the general catalog. Also, catalogs for other types of format collections are often separate and contain varying types of bibliographic information presented in different ways from that for book material. Some nonprint collections are oriented toward a specific type of user. These might include a music collection containing printed and manuscript music and sound recordings in different types of formats, such as discs and tapes, intended for the music researcher. Another type of nonprint collection for a client group would be a picture collection used by picture researchers in publishing and related media industries. Large picture collections are usually accessed by a unifaceted subject arrangement with cross references. For these materials, often no bibliographic record exists beyond that which is found on the item itself. There are many other examples of this type of nonprint collection which may be quite large and adequately serve the needs of the special user.

Two-year and community college libraries which collect instructional materials often have an omnimedia approach to bibliographic access. Academic libraries, on the other hand, unless they have adopted the media center pattern of collection development and service, usually handle their nonprint materials by dividing them into a number of special collections, much like the medium-sized and large public library with special nonprint collections. Music, art history, film, oral history, and other special collections with bibliographic access different from that for print materials, are common in academic libraries. Media collections also exist as parts of other special collections in colleges and universities. One or several formats such as film, sound recordings, and videotape may be a part of a law library, a medical school library, a college of education curriculum library, or other departmental library. In each instance, the bibliographic records for the nonprint may or may not be integrated with the records for books. In an academic library, book material is often processed centrally, whereas nonprint may be cataloged by someone in the special collection.

USER NEEDS

The pivotal point in making decisions about a system for providing bibliographic control of nonprint in a service agency, such as a library or media center, is the core of users' needs for bibliographic information. Those who catalog nonprint materials must understand not only the physical characteristics and the content of the material, but also the types and amount of information that the user will need to identify the material. Many libraries would benefit from reviewing their service objectives and considering the potential uses for the media materials which they currently collect. Also, many libraries might find that nonprint formats should receive a larger proportion of library budgets if the needs of the user for materials in all formats were given due consideration. User studies of current collections and surveys of the media needs of library users will aid the librarians who are responsible for collection development policies, as well as the cataloger concerned with bibliographic access to the library's media collection.

Unfortunately, perhaps, media collections have often developed with a specific and rather narrow view of the potential use of the material, and with a limited view of the many types of potential users who would benefit from bibliographic and physical access to all materials in the collection. School library media centers, in particular, have suffered from the assumption that because their major users are children, limited and simplified bibliographic information, provided in simplistic cataloging, is all that is necessary. Many schools use cataloging manuals which do justice neither to the materials nor to the patrons who need more and better information about materials in the collections. On the other end of the spectrum, special research collections may provide extensive bibliographic information about the materials but record it in such a way that only the specialized user can understand the catalog entry. When special collections are accessed only through special and different catalogs, access to the material for the general user may be short circuited. A picture researcher, for example, wanting to find a detail of a reproduction of a certain painting will need to have specific facts about the item recorded in the catalog entry in order to uniquely identify the item. A child wanting to find a picture of a still life to copy in art class, however, may find an entirely different use for the item and could benefit by a different type of access to the same item. An art reproduction which would meet both needs might be found in a large picture collection of a special, academic, or public library, as well as a school library media center.

As multi-type library cooperation and resource sharing become more important in library service, the concept of the "library user" for any given agency will be redefined to include all potential users of the cooperating institutions. School collections will be used by adult, general, and specialized users, and children will have access to materials in specialized nonprint collections in other types of libraries. Standardization of the bibliographic record and the provision of sufficient, accurate information for all library users in cataloging information which is to be shared between and among different types of libraries will increase the use of nonprint materials by increasing their accessibility to all types of library patrons. *AACR 2* provides rules for bibliographic description adequate for many different types of uses and users of the formats which it includes. With the exception of large, heavily used, special collections which have developed sophisticated methods for cataloging materials adequate for those whom they choose to serve, the type of bibliographic description provided by *AACR 2* may have real advantages for the user.

CATALOGING PRACTICES PRIOR TO AACR 2

Concern about providing bibliographic access to nonprint materials in library collections has been evident in the library profession for more than 50 years. A chronology of events relevant to the history of cataloging nonprint is presented in *Project Media Base: Final Report to the National Commission on Libraries and Information Science.*[6] The early history reveals a focus on motion pictures, particularly educational motion pictures. In 1951, the Library of Congress took the early lead in developing cataloging rules for motion pictures and filmstrips based on rules developed by the Copyright Office in 1946. In the 1950s and 1960s, LC published supplements to their basic rules for descriptive cataloging which covered, in addition to motion pictures, phonorecords, pictures, designs, and other two-dimensional representations. Since 1953, films and other materials for projection, plus music, books on music, and sound recordings, have been included in Library of Congress catalogs. See the Bibliography of Cataloging Aids (Appendix I) at the end of this text for citations for the LC catalogs containing copy of catalog records for nonprint materials.

In 1955, the American Library Association appointed a Special Committee on the Bibliographic Control of Audiovisual Materials. The report of this committee, issued in 1957, suggested standardization of essential bibliographic elements for nonprint and the publication of a manual for cataloging nonprint material. Although the formats differ greatly, there are elements common to their nature that can be grouped into areas for description. Generally, they include:

Medium designation: the family of materials to which the item belongs

Title: the title of the media package and titles of the parts

Responsibility: those individuals and groups who contribute to the concept and making of the item and those responsible for performance

Publication: individuals and groups responsible for production, publication, manufacturing, and distribution

Dates: of production, publication, and copyright

Physical description: details about the format of a single item or formats included in a multipart item

Series: the group of publications to which the item belongs

Summary: objective description of content

Intended audience: groups and age levels for which the item is appropriate

Availability: standard number or ordering number

Notes: additional information explaining or qualifying any of the above.

Information in these general categories is necessary for almost any library user. In determining how much and what information within each of the categories is necessary in a given collection, the nature of the material itself and the user should be considered in applying a cataloging code. Inclusion of a standard for description of all nonprint formats in a cataloging code did not become a reality until the publication of *AACR 2* in 1978, however. Prior to that time, librarians and media specialists faced difficult problems in choosing and applying cataloging rules to media materials.

Many libraries, particularly academic, research, and public libraries, followed LC practice and used LC cards for the materials which were cataloged by that agency. LC rules were the basis of the rules for cataloging nonprint materials presented in the first edition of the *Anglo-American Cataloging Rules* (Chicago: American Library Association, 1967), and libraries already using LC cataloging adopted the first edition, applying the rules presented there for some or all of the formats which *AACR 1* covers. Included in Part III of *AACR 1* are rules for manuscripts; maps, atlases, etc.; motion pictures and filmstrips; music, including uniform titles; phonorecords; and pictures, designs, and other two-dimensional representations. Chapter 12 of *AACR 1*, which covers motion pictures and filmstrips, was revised and expanded to include other formats and was published in 1975. It includes "principal audiovisual media" defined as motion pictures, filmstrips, videorecordings, slides, transparencies, and certain other materials viewed as instructional aids. These aids are charts, dioramas, flash cards, games, kits, microscope slides, models, and realia. Chapter 14 of *AACR 1* which contains the rules for phonorecords was revised and published in 1976 under the title "Sound Recordings." Most libraries using *AACR 1* adopted the revised chapters covering nonprint materials. Chapter 11, for maps and atlases, and Chapter 15, for pictures, etc. were not revised prior to *AACR 2*. It was necessary to use the basic *AACR 1* volume and the revised chapters in dealing with nonprint formats.

Revised Chapter 6 of *AACR 1* which was based on the International Standard Bibliographic Description (Monographs) was published in 1974. It did not accommodate nonprint materials, however. Neither Revised Chapter 12 nor Revised Chapter 14 incorporate a standard bibliographic description for nonprint, although the rules do bring the elements of description more closely in line with the standard elements for book material.

In the 1960s and early 1970s large numbers of nonprint materials were being produced, mainly for the educational market, and were being collected by school library media centers. Most school media specialists found the rules for cataloging nonprint in the first edition of the *Anglo-American Cataloging Rules* inappropriate and inadequate for their purposes. Schools were collecting materials in all formats and were looking for cataloging guidelines which would allow the bibliographic records for all material to be integrated in an omnimedia catalog. *AACR 1* was very uneven in its treatment of nonprint formats and did not even include rules for some of the formats which schools were collecting. Media specialists also complained that the rules for nonprint in *AACR 1* were intended for research libraries which required a more complete bibliographic record than schools required. Some school libraries used *AACR 1* and later the revised chapters of those rules, but many adopted other guidelines which provided rules for all of the formats which they collected.

In response to the need for cataloging rules which covered more educational formats and provided simplified rules appropriate for school media centers, a number of individual authors and groups published cataloging rules for nonprint. As might be expected, many state departments of education and some state library or media associations sponsored publication of cataloging guidelines for nonprint materials in schools. State or local guidelines for cataloging were published and used by school libraries in Arizona, California, Kentucky, Michigan, New York, North Carolina, and Wisconsin. These publications were circulated and used in other states as well.

One of the earliest and most popular of these guides which was published in 1967, the same year in which *AACR 1* was published, was a *Cataloging Manual for Nonbook Materials in Learning Centers and School Libraries* by Judith Westhuis. It is typical of the type of cataloging aid available and adopted by schools at that time. It was written as a guide for a public school system and published by the Michigan Association of School Librarians. The 36 page booklet is a cataloging and processing manual and includes directions for locally adopted procedures. It lacks a statement of cataloging principles and provides few general rules. The cataloger is left to infer the rules from the examples given of cataloging for the various formats. It does not group the formats according to common physical characteristics, but instead gives different guidelines for each type of format. Guidelines for each of the formats do include rules for some of the basic bibliographic elements such as title and imprint, and a suggestion is made for main entry for each format. These are not consistent from format to format, however. A method for physical description of each format is also included. Practices used in the school system such as color coding of catalog cards and the inclusion of media symbols in the call number are also suggested. Given the problems associated with *AACR 1*, school media specialists saw certain advantages to adopting a manual such as this. All of the formats which they collected were covered. The guidelines produced simple bibliographic records, and help was given in processing and labeling the materials, tasks which had presented an additional challenge.

The simple nature of this manual, however, belies the complex nature of the task. Unless the item in hand is essentially the same as the example of the format given, the rules are not adequate to cover the bibliographic facts. Lacking a standard description for all formats, each format is handled differently, resulting in bibliographic records which differ in the amount and type of information given for various formats. Rules for entry are also inconsistent.

Another publication which attempted to simplify the task of cataloging nonprint material is *AV Cataloging and Processing Simplified* by Jean Thornton Johnson, et al. (Raleigh, North Carolina: Audiovisual Catalogers, 1971). Again, this is the product of the work of librarians in a school system, attempting to devise methods for solving the problems encountered in trying to catalog their collections. Much like the Michigan rules discussed above, this manual approaches the task by media format, with each of the 20 chapters devoted to a format type. They include:

Art Prints
Charts
Film Loops
Films
Filmstrips
Filmstrips with Sound
Flashcards
Globes
Kits
Maps
Microforms
Models
Pictures
Realia
Records
Slides
Study Prints
Tape Recordings
Transparencies
Videotapes

This 236 page manual is much broader in its coverage than some of the other manuals available at that time. For each format, instructions are given for cataloging which include suggestions to use the Dewey Decimal Classification and *Sears List of Subject Headings.* This manual also provides individual directions for descriptive cataloging for each format. The descriptive cataloging includes information to be presented in the title paragraph, collation and series paragraph, notes, and tracings. Content of the cataloging entry is described simply in phrases, and each of the 20 format sections includes one example with main entry, subject entry, added entry, and shelflist card. Also included are extensive illustrations of practical processing and storing procedures and a cataloging worksheet. The worksheet introduces an intermediate step between the item and preparation of the catalog entry.

In terms of the overall effectiveness of the manual, however, many problems which the cataloger faces have not been addressed. Again, there are no general rules for entry and no consistent rules for choice and presentation of title information. Little guidance is given about publication statements, and although some detail is called for in the collation, the directions do not cover the many possible situations found in the format. Many of the suggestions for the processing and storage of materials are helpful; however, the confusion between physical and bibliographic access is apparent. The strength of this publication is in its inclusion of the preparation of materials for circulation. The ways in which materials are labeled, shelved, and circulated are very important; however, the ability of the user to identify an item and learn its characteristics in order to determine if it is useful for a given purpose is more basic. None of the rules published by state or local library associations, or by school systems or districts adequately address the basic problems of bibliographic access.

In an attempt to expand the coverage of cataloging rules and to provide some standard approach to cataloging nonprint materials for omnimedia collections, several national professional organizations sponsored the publication of rules or guidelines in the late 1960s and 1970s. The Library Association in conjunction with the National Council for Educational Technology published rules used in Great Britain.[7] In consultation with several associations in the United States and Canada, the Canadian Library Association published rules used in Canada and the United States.[8] The Association for Educational Communication and Technology (AECT), which was formerly part of the National Education Association in this country, published rules which were adopted by many schools in the United States.[9] In 1977, a survey of state school media supervisors in the 50 states and the District of Columbia revealed that only one-fifth of the state supervisors noted the use of *AACR 1* and its revisions in school libraries in their states. Seventeen state supervisors reported use of the first edition of the Canadian rules. The code used in most states in 1977 was the fourth edition of the AECT rules.[10] These cataloging codes and manuals continue to have an impact on bibliographic control of nonprint materials in school media center collections. Although these codes and manuals are an improvement over those published by other groups and individuals during those years, none of them incorporate the standard bibliographic description which is the basis of *AACR 2*. Unless media specialists adopt *AACR 2*, they will remain outside the bibliographic mainstream by continuing practices which are not compatible with the International Standard Bibliographic Description.

FOOTNOTES

1. National Center for Educational Statistics, *A Handbook of Standard Terminology and a Guide for Recording and Reporting Information about Educational Technology* (Washington, DC: Government Printing Office, 1975), p. iii.

2. Ibid., pp. 18-19.

3. *Media Programs: District and School* (Chicago: American Library Association, 1975), p. 44.

4. Ibid., p. 47.

5. Ibid., pp. 45-46.

6. *Problems in Bibliographic Access to Non-print Materials* (Washington, DC: National Commission on Libraries and Information Science, 1979), pp. 52-77.

7. Library Association Media Cataloging Rules Committee, *Non-book Materials Cataloguing Rules: An Integrated Code of Practice and Draft Revision of the Anglo-American Cataloguing Rules in British Text, Part III* (London: National Council for Educational Technology, 1973).

8. There are three editions of rules known as the "Canadian rules." The preliminary edition and the first edition are not based on a standard description. The 1979 or second edition is based on *AACR 2*. They are:

    Jean Riddle, Shirley Lewis, and Janet Macdonald, *Nonbook Materials: The Organization of Integrated Collections*, Preliminary ed. (Ottawa, ON: Canadian Library Association, 1970).

Jean Riddle Weihs, Shirley Lewis, and Janet Macdonald, *Nonbook Materials: The Organization of Integrated Collections* (Ottawa, ON: Canadian Library Association, 1973).

Jean Weihs with Shirley Lewis and Janet Macdonald, *Nonbook Materials: The Organization of Integrated Collections* (Ottawa, ON: Canadian Library Association, 1979).

9. There are four editions of the AECT code, none of which incorporate a standard description. They are:

Standards for Cataloging, Coding, and Scheduling Educational Media (Washington, DC: National Education Association, Department of Audiovisual Instruction, 1968).

Standards for Cataloging Nonprint Materials, 2nd ed. (Washington, DC: Association for Educational Communications and Technology, 1971).

Standards for Cataloging Nonprint Materials, 3rd ed. (Washington, DC: Association for Educational Communications and Technology, 1972).

Alma M. Tillin and William J. Quinly, *Standards for Cataloging Nonprint Materials*, 4th ed. (Washington, DC: Association for Educational Communications and Technology, 1976).

10. JoAnn V. Rogers, "Nonprint Cataloging: A Call for Standardization," *American Libraries* 10 (January 1979): 46-48.

II
AACR 2 and Nonprint Materials

AACR 2 PART 1. DESCRIPTION: INTRODUCTION

0.21.

Reflecting the change in emphasis from entry and headings, which were considered first and in great length in *AACR 1*, to bibliographic description of library materials, which is considered first and in much more detail in *AACR 2*, this code begins with rules for description. The Introduction to Part I and the first chapter, Chapter 1. General Rules for Description, relate to all types of materials, both print and nonprint. Selected general rules from Chapter 1 which are of particular importance in the description of nonprint will be discussed in this text.

0.22.

The framework on which the rules in this code is based is noted in this section of the Introduction. Providing a standard format within which all materials can be described, the General International Standard Bibliographic Description ISBD(G) is of prime importance to catalogers of nonprint. Adoption of this standard reflects the realization by the library profession that modifications were needed in the standard developed to provide bibliographic information for monographs, the International Standard Bibliographic Description for Monographic Publications ISBD(M), to accommodate nonprint materials. It also reflects the realization that although special standards may be desirable for the description of nonprint in special libraries, a general standard should be the basis for any additional descriptive formats which are developed for nonprint. The rules in *AACR 2* follow the general standard in two important aspects — the order of elements and their prescribed punctuation.

The following outline in Fig. 2-1 presents the ISBD(G) framework. The optional elements appearing in italics represent some of the modifications of ISBD(M) necessary to accommodate nonprint.

0.24.

The method of procedure that is to be followed in describing nonprint materials is to first apply the rules in the chapter dealing with the type of format to which the item belongs. This means that the cataloger determines the class of materials to which the item in hand belongs according to the physical characteristics of the item and goes immediately to the relevant chapter. As mentioned in 0.23., several parts of the rules may be used in recording the bibliographic information. Individual chapters for nonprint will refer the cataloger to the general rules in Part I, Chapter 1, and other chapters in Part I may also be needed. The form of the item in hand is the basis for the description, although notes can be given which provide information about the original.

Fig. 2-1.
ISBD(G)
International Standard Bibliographic Description (General)

Area	Prescribed Preceding (or Enclosing) Punctuation for Elements	Element	
Note: Each area, other than the first, is preceded by a point, space, dash, space (. —).			
1. **Title and statement of responsibility area**		1.1	Title proper
	[ ]	1.2	General material designation
	=	1.3	Parallel title
	:	1.4	Other title information
		1.5	Statements of responsibility
	/		First statement
	;		Subsequent statement
2. **Edition area**		2.1	Edition statement
	=	2.2	Parallel edition statement
		2.3	Statements of responsibility relating to the edition
	/		First statement
	;		Subsequent statement
	,	2.4	Additional edition statement
		2.5	Statements of responsibility following an additional edition statement
	/		First statement
	;		Subsequent statement
3. **Material (or type of publication) specific details area**			
4. **Publication, distribution, etc., area**		4.1	Place of Publication, distribution, etc.
			First place
	;		Subsequent place
	:	4.2	Name of publisher, distributor, etc.
	[ ]	4.3	Statement of function of publisher, distributor, etc.
4. **Publication, distribution, etc., area**	,	4.4	Date of publication, distribution, etc.
	(	4.5	Place of manufacture
	:	4.6	Name of manufacturer
	,)	4.7	Date of manufacture

(Figure continues on page 32)

Fig. 2-1 (cont'd)

Area	Prescribed Preceding (or Enclosing) Punctuation for Elements	Element
5. **Physical description area**		5.1 Specific material designation and extent of item
	:	5.2 Other physical details
	;	5.3 Dimensions of item
	+	5.4 Accompanying material statement
6. **Series area**		6.1 Title proper of series
Note: A series statement is	=	6.2 Parallel title of series
enclosed by parentheses.	:	6.3 Other title information of series
When there are two or		
more series statements,		6.4 Statements of responsibility relating to the series
each is enclosed in		
parentheses.	/	First statement
	;	Subsequent statement
	,	6.5 International Standard Serial Number of series
	;	6.6 Numbering within series
	.	6.7 Enumeration and/or title of subseries
	=	6.8 Parallel title of subseries
	:	6.9 Other title information of subseries
		6.10 Statements of responsibility relating to the subseries
	/	First statement
	;	Subsequent statement
		6.11 International Standard Serial Number of subseries
	;	6.12 Numbering within subseries
7. **Note area**		
8. **Standard number (or alternative) and terms of availability area**		8.1 Standard number (or alternative)
	=	8.2 Key title
	:	8.3 Terms of availability and/or price
	( )	8.4 Qualification (in varying positions)

SOURCE: International Federation of Library Associations. Working Group on the General International Bibliographic Description. *ISBD(G): General International Standard Bibliographic Description: Annotated Text.* London: IFLA International Office for UBC, 1977, pp. 2-3.

0.27.

The use of notes for which rules are given in individual chapters for nonprint are to be considered optional. The greatly expanded coverage of the types of notes appropriate for nonprint materials is a great help to the cataloger in determining types of information to be given and in determining the order of presentation of the information. Liberal use of notes, suggested in the rules, will increase the probability that needed information will appear in the catalog record.

0.29.

The first mention of another important provision of this code, the three levels of description, is made here. This rule gives libraries license to use the same level for all materials or to use different levels of description for different types of materials. The suggestion that libraries adopt guidelines about the use of the various levels is one that should be followed. Each library should set policies concerning levels of description based on those considerations discussed in Chapter I of this text: the type of collection, the needs of the users, and the probability that cataloging records for materials in the collection will be shared in a bibliographic utility or other type of cooperative venture. Although librarians, especially those dealing with small collections and general rather than sophisticated, specialized users in school libraries and small public libraries may be attracted by the simplicity of the first level of description, this level does not do justice to the nature of most nonprint material. Also, it should be considered that the second level of description is the minimum level acceptable for entry of catalog records into the shared records of bibliographic utilities.

The first provision of this rule should be carefully considered. It specifies that the information required by each of the levels is to be considered a minimum. The cataloger may choose the first or second level of description and selectively add information deemed necessary for the item and for the users of the collection. The cataloger can record all of the data in the elements dictated by the first level and selectively add information, according to the rules, to be applied to materials being cataloged on the more specific levels two and three. Without some guidelines, this provision can lead to a great deal of variation in the amount and types of data given by different catalogers working with the same level of description. Consistent use of the second level of description could avoid problems associated with the need to always make decisions on a case-by-case basis.

Additional discussion of the levels of description appear in this text under rule 1.0D.

AACR 2 CHAPTER 1: GENERAL RULES FOR DESCRIPTION

1.0. GENERAL RULES

The general rules given in the first chapter are applicable to all types of materials. When the item in hand necessitates more specific directions, as is usually the case with nonprint materials, the rules in subsequent chapters of Part I, applicable to the type of format being cataloged, supersede and/or supplement the general rules presented here. It should be remembered that according to 0.24. the description should be based on the rules in the chapter dealing with the class of material to which the item belongs.

1.0A. SOURCES OF INFORMATION

This first general rule illustrates the above point. It instructs the cataloger to consult a specific chapter in Part I to determine the sources of information for the description. It announces that each chapter will define the chief source of information for the type of item, will often rank in order of preference other sources of information, and will prescribe sources of information for each area of the description. A general rule is that information taken from outside the prescribed sources used in the description should be enclosed in square brackets.

Items which lack suggested sources of information can have the information supplied by the cataloger, with an indication in the notes of the source of the information and explanation of the source if it is not evident from the description. The note often found on LC copy "Titles supplied from data sheet" illustrates this rule. Because the cataloger does not have the item in hand, and the title is taken from a source other than the chief source, the item itself, this information is given in a note. Catalogers making use of LC copy should realize that most of the cataloging of audiovisual materials done at LC is from data sheets containing information usually supplied by the publisher of the material. In October 1981, the Audiovisual Section of the Descriptive Cataloging Division became a part of the new Special Materials Cataloging Division which includes audiovisual, manuscripts, and music sections plus rare book catalogers. Although one would hope for increased emphasis from LC on cataloging of nonprint in this new division, the process which does not allow for examination of the item in hand by the audiovisual catalogers has not yet had a chance to evolve. Cataloging from data sheets with information supplied by people unfamiliar with rules for extracting bibliographic information from the item puts LC catalogers at a great disadvantage. One can only hope that this situation will change.

The first challenge faced by the cataloger with a nonprint item in hand is to determine accurate and appropriate bibliographic information from the item. As anyone who has worked with nonprint materials knows, extracting this information can be a problem. Nonprint materials do not have title pages giving complete and succinct bibliographic information. Pieces of information must be assembled from many sources, including relevant parts of the item itself, labels, containers, study guides, etc. Many problems arise because of the labeling of the item and the way in which bibliographic information is given by the producers and publishers. Inaccurate, incomplete, and conflicting information can be found in single part items. Problems are compounded when the nonprint material contains several parts, as many of them do.

The rules given in each chapter for determining sources of information for the various areas and elements of the description are intended to aid in providing a consistent and unique description for each item cataloged. According to the mnemonic numbering system, rules in each chapter which are preceded by the chapter number and followed by .0B1. define and limit the locations which can be considered the chief source of information. In some instances, the chief source is limited to one location while in others, several locations are acceptable. Rules in each chapter preceded by the chapter number and followed by .0B2. indicate which source or sources can be used in finding descriptive information for each of the areas of the description. Because of the differences in the materials themselves, the chief source(s) and other sources of information differ greatly from chapter to chapter. A careful reading of these instructions should be the first step in constructing a catalog record.

A few general guidelines are given in Chapter I, Rule 1.0H. for items with several chief sources of information. For single part items with several chief sources of information, use the first occurring chief source except:

a. with a sound recording, treat two or more chief sources as one source (also Rule 6.0B1.).

b. with conflicting chief sources bearing different dates of publication, distribution, etc., use the source bearing the most recent date.

c. when cataloging parts of a multipart item singly, choose the chief source according to that information which relates to the single item being cataloged.

Two other parts of the rule deal with language or script. For multipart items, use information found in the chief source for the first part. If there is no first part, choose a source which gives the most information, or, as last resort, use a unifying element. The various sources used as chief sources of information for different parts of the description can be indicated in notes. If the other chapters in Part I are inconsistent with these general directions, the instructions in the chapter related to the item in hand, once again, are the rules which take precedence.

Problems still exist with these rules as outlined in *AACR 2*. The rules for determining the chief source of information are not always clear, and in some cases, the chief source as prescribed is not really the best source for finding the most accurate information. In the chapter on film, for example, directions are given to use the film itself and the title frames or the container if the container is an integral part. Only the cataloger's familiarity with the format can help in determining the information to be used within the framework of the intent of the directions. A film enclosed in a cartridge with one title or form of the title appearing on the cassette, another form of the title on beginning title frames, and another appearing on final frames leaves the cataloger with a choice, even within the rules for prescribed sources of information. In this instance, the producers catalog or accompanying material, which may indicate the title chosen by the producer or publisher of the film, could be used to determine which of the sources carries the title assigned to the item by the groups or individuals responsible for its content.

The importance of viewing or listening to materials and examining all parts of a multipart item should be understood by those individuals cataloging media. Although the rules give guidance in suggesting places to look for information, they cannot reconcile conflicting information given in various sources to help in determining which information is the most appropriate for the description. This is where the cataloger's understanding of the nature of the formats and the ways in which media producers and publishers put together and label nonprint materials come into play. A good descriptive catalog entry demands an understanding of the type of format being described, as well as the ability to locate relevant rules and to apply them accurately.

Catalogers should also be alert to the fact that many sources of cataloging copy contain bibliographic records which are not based on information derived from the item in hand, but instead from information supplied to the cataloging agency by the producer or other intermediary. This is true of copy from the

Library of Congress and from the National Information Center for Educational Media (NICEM). Often looked to by other libraries as an authoritative source of information for bibliographic records, these agencies may, in fact, produce records which are less accurate in their choice of information than a cataloger, who is working with the item in hand, can find and use. If the cataloger wants to construct the best possible record corresponding to the item in hand, the problems associated with the sources of information available to the agency doing the original cataloging will have to be considered. The cataloger should determine if the best sources of information yield the bibliographic data that is given by other cataloging agencies.

Because of the large number and diverse types of formats, and because of the different content contained in the various nonprint formats, another challenge is offered to the nonprint cataloger—to have available reference sources for different formats which will aid in constructing a complete and accurate description. The item and a copy of the rules are not enough. When bibliographic information is presented in conflicting forms and when needed information is totally missing for an item, other sources must be used in order to complete an entry. The rules for prescribed sources of information for the areas of the description allow use of "any source" for several areas, often including the physical description, the notes, the standard number, and terms of availability. One type of source which is helpful with all types of nonprint formats is a file of catalogs from producers, publishers, manufacturers, and distributors. Because retrospective cataloging, as well as cataloging of currently produced materials, will take place in most libraries, these files should contain retrospective as well as current catalogs.

Other sources which assist the cataloger are reference materials which contain information concerning groups, individuals, companies, and associations related to the production and publication of nonprint. These too should be retrospective and current. Some of these sources are listed in a bibliography at the end of the text (Appendix V). Also, as previously mentioned, catalogers do rely on catalog copy from other library agencies. However, the information provided in catalog copy should always be checked against the item itself.

1.0B. ORGANIZATION OF THE DESCRIPTION

The areas into which the descriptive elements are organized are dictated by ISBD(G), summarized under rule 0.22. in this text. The terms used in the ISBD(G) frameword are general and apply to print and nonprint bibliographic information. Instead of author, title, publisher, collation, etc. the terms now cover different types of bibliographic information relevant to nonprint. The first area, .1, is designated as the TITLE AND STATEMENT OF RESPONSIBILITY AREA. Those individuals and groups responsible for nonprint material extend well beyond the relationship between author and printed work, and the change in terminology reflects this fact. Several other areas retain formerly used terminology and are appropriate for book and nonbook materials alike. These include .2 EDITION AREA, .6 SERIES AREA, and .7 NOTE AREA. One of the most helpful features of *AACR 2* for the nonprint catalogers is the expansion of consideration of notes appropriate to different media formats. As we shall see, notes are discussed in each of the chapters devoted to nonprint. Rules for choosing information for notes for each type of format, order of notes, and some suggestions for formulation of notes (1.7A3. Form of notes) provide effective guidelines for giving important information which is not included in the body of the description. Liberal use of notes, even when using the first level of description, can solve many problems which nonprint materials inherently present.

Four other areas also demonstrate the accommodation of nonprint. These include .3 MATERIAL (OR TYPE OF PUBLICATION) SPECIFIC DETAILS AREA, an area used with cartographic material. One of the most significant areas for nonprint is the .5 PHYSICAL DESCRIPTION AREA where many of the characteristics of the physical entity can be described in a standard way. Formerly called the collation, this area can now include many specific details to help the user determine the type of equipment needed to use the item. Coordination of the information given here with notes about physical characteristics are noteworthy contributions of the new rules. The last area .8 STANDARD NUMBER AND TERMS OF AVAILABILITY provides a designated area in the description in which standard identifying numbers, such as the International Standard Book Number (ISBN), can be recorded. In the absence of an international standard numbering system for nonprint materials, a rule in each chapter under .7B19. accommodates nonprint by providing a space in the notes for single numbers for one item or several numbers for a multipart item. These numbers also can be an aid in differentiating parts of sets and series of nonprint materials. It is an important piece of information and should be included in most instances. This rule also indicates that each of the areas is divided into various elements. The detailed instructions for recording pertinent elements, particularly in the physical description, is a great improvement in the description of nonprint.

1.0C. PUNCTUATION

Rules for punctuation are found in several places in *AACR 2*, including general rule 1.0C. and rules for punctuation in each area found in Chapter I. They are:

1.0.   General Rules
   1.0C.   Punctuation

1.1.   Title and Statement of Responsibility Area
   1.1A1. Punctuation

1.2.   Edition Area
   1.2A1. Punctuation

1.3.   Material (or Type of Publication) Specific Details Area

1.4.   Publication, Distribution, etc., Area
   1.4A1. Punctuation

1.5.   Physical Description Area
   1.5A1. Punctuation

1.6.   Series Area
   1.6A1. Punctuation

1.7.   Note Area
   1.7A1. Punctuation

1.8.   Standard Number and Terms of Availability Area
   1.8A1. Punctuation

Rules for punctuation are given in each chapter under the mnemonic structure consisting of the chapter number and the area number, followed by A1. All of these rules must be considered by the cataloger. General rules include the use of a period, space, dash, space between areas, or the use of a new paragraph to begin an area. All marks of prescribed punctuation are preceded by a space and followed by a space, with the exception of the comma and the period. The hyphen, parenthesis, and square brackets are not preceded or followed by a space. Other generalities are discussed in Rule 1.0C. With names of the elements representing their content, punctuation for a typical nonprint entry on the third level would be as indicated below:

Title proper [general material designation] = parallel title : other title information / first statement of responsibility ; subsequent statement of responsibility. — edition statement / first statement of responsibility relating to the edition ; subsequent statement of responsibility relating to the edition. — first place of publication, distribution, etc. : name of publisher, distributor [optional statement of function of publisher, distributor] ; subsequent place of publication, distribution, etc. : subsequent name of publisher, distributor [optional statement of function] , date of publication (place of manufacture : name of manufacturer)

Extent of item including specific material designation : other physical details ; dimensions + accompanying material — (Series statement = parallel series statement, standard serial numbering of series. sub-series statement = parallel sub-series statement, standard serial numbering of sub-series ; numbering within sub-series)

Notes

Standard number or alternative terms of availability and/or price.

1.0D.   LEVELS OF DESCRIPTION
The elements to be included in each of the three levels of description are outlined in 1.0D. It should be remembered that the elements set forth for each level are the minimum set, all of which must be used when applying the chosen level. In addition, other elements can be added to any level. All of the information included in whatever level is chosen should be included in the bibliographic entry if the information is applicable to the item in hand.

1.0D1.   First level of description
Because of its simplicity, libraries with small collections and limited use may want to consider adoption of this level. It includes title; statement of responsibility, only if in a form that is different from the main entry or if the item is given a title entry; edition; and publisher and date in the body of the entry. The physical description need include only the extent of the item, which consists of a number of physical items and a specific medium designator such as "6 filmstrips." It also includes notes, which in the case of nonprint items would include the number borne by the item. This level also includes area .3 for cartographic materials, if applicable.

Libraries used mainly by children may find some factors to recommend using this level. For example, it is the least confusing for a reader with a low level of comprehension and is certainly easy for the cataloger. Missing from the description, however, is much information which might be helpful for teachers, parents, and librarians working with the children. The record also omits information which would be useful to other professional staff.

This level omits the general material designation which, coming immediately after the title, provides an early indication to the user that the item is not print. This early warning alerts the user that equipment may be needed to use the item. It omits statements of responsibility which can aid the teacher in determining the authority of the material contained in the items. It omits the place of publication which can aid librarians in locating reorder information. It includes only the first named agency responsible for publication and may omit other publication information which is significant for the unique identification of an item associated with more than one publisher. The physical description does not prescribe inclusion of all of the information needed for the user to be able to determine the type of equipment needed to use the item. All or any of these elements can be selectively added to level one or can be explained in notes. The body of the entry, where many catalog users stop reading, however, omits much useful information. Also, if information omitted from the body of the entry is assigned to the notes, the information can be given in a much less formal and predictable manner which is often more confusing for the user than inclusion of this information in a prescribed manner in the body of the entry.

From the cataloger's point of view, trying to determine which information and how much information omitted from the body should be included in the notes, on an item-by-item basis, necessitates making many decisions about contents and form of notes for each item. Using level one may result in more work and less uniform catalog records. This can be avoided by choosing a level which prescribes more detail in the first place.

1.0D2. Second level of description
The second level prescribes most of the elements necessary for the unique identification of nonprint items. Missing from level one, but included in level two is the general material designation. This list of nonprint material types or categories is found in 1.1C1. As previously mentioned, chief obstacles to uniformity in nonprint cataloging have been the different categorization of media materials in cataloging codes and manuals, and the different terminology applied to generic and specific categories of nonprint media. *AACR 2* gives us a national and international standard which should be applied in bibliographic description. Continued variation from these standard terms can only breed continued confusion on the part of the library user.

Reflecting the development and use of different terms to describe media types on both sides of the Atlantic, *AACR 2* lists two sets of general material designations. One is British and the other is the North American grouping of materials which corresponds to the more general British categories. This approach is the result of many compromises. Upon first consideration by North American catalogers, it may not seem to represent the best of all possible worlds. The list, when combined with the specific materials designation given in the physical description and notes clarifying specifics of the physical characteristics of the item, does enable catalogers to provide a universally understood standard description of media materials.

Several other elements, important for the identification of nonprint and omitted from level one, are included in level two. Statements of responsibility, those individuals and groups responsible for the intellectual and artistic content of nonprint, are often very important to nonprint materials and should be included in the body of the entry, rather than be relegated to the notes. A statement of responsibility related to the edition may aid in unique identification of the item for the user and should be included. Place of publication and other publication information, omitted from level one, can be useful also.

The most important difference between level one and level two for nonprint is probably the expanded physical description prescribed in level two. Physical details about the item are necessary to inform the user about the nature of the item which determines the type of equipment needed for its use. Information about dimensions of some nonprint formats is also needed in order to determine the way in which materials can be used. Series information, particularly when parts of a set of materials are divided and cataloged separately with the set designated as the series, is also necessary for identification. Both series title and number are needed in the catalog record. Level two will be the level which almost all libraries containing nonprint materials will want to use for these materials.

1.0D3. Third level of description

Some libraries may want to use level three for all of their nonprint; others may want to use it for only selected types of formats. Most libraries will want to adopt level two and add selectively from rules which supplement the information prescribed in level two. The addition of information from rules used only in level three should be determined by user needs and the nature of the bibliographic information related to the material.

1.0H. ITEMS WITH SEVERAL CHIEF SOURCES OF INFORMATION

This rule which is an important one for some nonprint formats is discussed in this text under 1.0A., Sources of information. It can be used in choosing one chief source over another as the basis for description in either single part or multipart items when there are no more specific or conflicting guidelines concerning the choice of chief sources in Chapters 3-11 of *AACR 2*. As with all other rules in Chapter 1 of *AACR 2*, if a more specific rule is provided in a chapter covering one of the formats being cataloged, the rule in the chapters covering the format takes precedence over a general rule in Chapter 1.

1.1. TITLE AND STATEMENT OF RESPONSIBILITY AREA

General rules indicate punctuation to be used in this area and instruct the cataloger to take information used from the chief source of information for the type of material being cataloged. Additional rules for choice of source of information are found in the various chapters under the menmonic numbers .0B1. and .0B2. It should be remembered that the rules for choice of source(s) of information found in the chapters for nonprint materials are to be considered first. The general rules given in this chapter can be used in the absence of a more specific rule for a nonprint format. Information which is not taken from one of the sources acceptable as a chief source for the title and statement of responsibility must be enclosed in brackets [ ]. Records for nonprint materials will often make use of information not within the chief source(s); therefore, brackets will often be found in this and other areas.

The title proper is the first element. It includes an alternative title (Rule 1.1B1.). If an item lacks title information in the prescribed chief source or sources of information, a title can be supplied from another part of the item or from any source in which a title can be found. If a title from a source other than the chief source must be used, the information should appear in brackets (Rule 1.1B7.). If the item lacks a title and no title can be found in reference sources, the cataloger supplies a title. It should be a descriptive word or short phrase using terms which indicate, in the most specific way possible, the nature of the material. Titles are often supplied for locally produced items and multipart items of three-dimensional material.

1.1C. OPTIONAL ADDITION. GENERAL MATERIAL DESIGNATION

The general material designation (GMD) appears in square brackets following the title proper and alternative title, but before parallel titles, those in other languages, and other title information or subtitles. This placement of the GMD for nonprint materials insures an early indication of the type of format. GMDs must be chosen from the list appearing in Rule 1.1C1., and the term is always given in the singular form. For nonprint materials they include:

map
globe

art original
chart
filmstrip
flash card
picture
slide
technical drawing
transparency

machine-readable data file

manuscript

microform

motion picture

kit

music

diorama
game
microscope slide
model
realia

sound recording

videorecording

The GMD is chosen to describe the format in hand. Materials originally published in another format or available in another format are not considered in choosing the designator. For example, materials in a microformat originally published in hard copy are cataloged, according to AACR 2, microforms. For modification of this rule see Chapter VIII of this text for more information. A graphic item appearing on a slide is generally categorized in the GMD as [slide] rather than [art original], [chart], etc. A kinescope recording is categorized as a videorecording rather than a film.

Rules concerning the use of the term "kit," discussed in the next few pages of the text, appear in the note following the list of GMDs in Rule 1.1C1. The distinction made here is the same as that found in the definition of terms in the *AACR 2* Glossary.

Each of the terms used as a GMD is defined briefly in the *AACR 2* Glossary, Appendix D. Reference to each definition can also be found in the *AACR 2* Index, which provides useful access if there is confusion about the term or the category of materials appropriate for the item in hand. The general material designation following the title proper and the specific material designation which appears in the first element of the physical description should work in concert to characterize the format and the extent of the format.

The first step in describing a nonprint item is to determine the GMD category and to determine which basic chapter of Part I should be used to describe the item. These decisions are made based on the glossary definition of GMD terms. The choice of GMDs will become standard if the definitions offered are carefully applied.

As mentioned in the *AACR 2* Introduction, it may be necessary to consult several chapters in formulating a descriptive entry. The basic chapter to be consulted is that one which contains rules for the type of material designated in the GMD; for example, for a motion picture the basic chapter would be Chapter 7. It will refer the cataloger to rules in Chapter 1, and other chapters may need to be consulted as well. These may include Chapter 12, if the item is part of a serial publication and Chapter 2, if the item is accompanied by monographic material which also warrants detailed description. If accompanied by another nonprint format, another of the chapters may also need to be consulted.

The terminology for the GMDs is standardized and must be given in the singular form exactly as listed in 1.1C. The specific material designations appropriately used with each of the GMDs are listed in each chapter covering nonprint materials. Most chapters provide a suggested list of specific terms which can be used, and many of these chapters allow the cataloger to supply a more specific term if none of the terms listed as suggested specific material designators apply to the item in hand. Each cataloging agency will have to make some decisions about the terms which are chosen for specific designators. One library may choose to consistently apply one of the suggested terms rather than choose others, while another library may want to use a combination of suggested terms and a few additional terms, the application of which is set in library policy. Another agency may, by choice or by default, leave the choice to the cataloger without internal guidelines. A logical starting point in the formulation of policies to guide the procedures in this and other matters would be the policy decisions made by the Library of Congress and recorded in the Library of Congress *Cataloging Service Bulletin.* See the bibliography of cataloging aids (Appendix I) listed at the end of the text for a reference to this and other cataloging tools.

Following is a list of definitions of terms which are used as GMDs and a discussion of the various specific designators which can be used in conjunction with each one. The definitions are taken from the *AACR 2* glossary. The specific designators and guidelines for the use of terms as specific designators, which are not listed, appear in the mnemonic numbering structure under each chapter number followed by .5, the PHYSICAL DESCRIPTION AREA, of which the specific designator is a part, and is followed by B1., which is the number for this element of description. The element is "Extent of the item (including specific material designation)." The GMDs in this discussion are listed alphabetically.

DEFINITIONS OF TERMS USED AS GMDs

[art original]

> The original two- or three-dimensional work of art (other than an art print (q.v.) or a photograph) created by the artist, e.g., a painting, a drawing, or sculpture, as contrasted with a reproduction of it.

The term is applied only to items created by the artist. An art print which is defined as "printed from the plate prepared by the artist" is given the GMD [picture]. This GMD is used for two-dimensional visuals to which a more specific term does not accurately apply. The GMD [picture] will be applied to many types of graphics that can be further described in the physical description which includes the specific designator.

In describing a two-dimensional art original, the cataloger is instructed to choose one of the terms listed in 8.5B1. The term, in most cases, would be the same as the GMD, but may be given in the plural. The optional rule which allows for the use of a more specific term can also be used. Particularly in a special library or one which collects a large number of different types of two-dimensional art, a more specific term may be desirable. They would include terms such as "woodcut," "painting," etc. The medium and the base given in other physical details can be used with either the given term or another term applied by the catalogers. Libraries with large collections or art originals and other graphics may also want to consider using the rules currently being developed by the Prints and Photographs Division of the Library of Congress. See Chapter VI of this text for a discussion of these rules.

Some confusion arises in the application of the GMD term to three-dimensional objects such as sculpture, which, because of physical characteristics, should be described according to rules in Chapter 10, Three-dimensional Artifacts and Realia. Using Chapter 10, the GMD would be [art original] and the specific designation would be covered in 10.5B1. which allows for use of several terms listed or a more specific name of the object. An original sculpture could be given the specific designator "sculpture" and be further described in other physical details according to the material from which the object is made; for example, 1 sculpture : bronze.

[chart]

> 1.   An opaque sheet that exhibits data in graphic or tabular form, e.g., a wall chart.   2.   In cartography, a special-purpose map....

When used as a GMD, this term in the North American list applies to graphic material. The term "map" is to be used for cartographic materials rather than "chart."

The specific terms suggested in 8.5B1. include "flip chart(s)" or "wall chart(s)," the two most common types. Other types can be described simply as "chart(s)."

[diorama]

> A three-dimensional representation of a scene created by placing objects, figures, etc., in front of a two-dimensional painted background.

Although the diorama is used as an exhibit in most cases, it is a more specific term and can be used in both the GMD and the specific designation. The fact that this term is used as a GMD reflects the fact that some GMDs apply to a broad category of materials, while others are fairly specific.

[filmstrip]

> A length of film containing a succession of images intended for projection one at a time, with or without recorded sound.

Single filmstrips, sets of filmstrips, and all types of filmstrips accompanied by sound recorded on disc, tape, or other sound format fall into this category. Because the visual component of a sound-filmstrip combination is thought to carry the burden of intellectual content and the sound is not intended to be used without the visual component, filmstrips accompanied by sound are categorized according to their graphic, visual base. See "kit" below for clarification of the use of that term in *AACR 2.*

"Filmslip(s)" and "filmstrip(s)" are two suggested terms which will be applicable to these materials. Rule 8.5C4. tells us to indicate, in other physical details, the presence of sound if it is integral, that is, found on the physical item, e.g., a filmstrip with a soundtrack. Most sound filmstrip presentations do not have integral sound, and the sound accompanying the filmstrip(s) is described as accompanying material elsewhere in the physical description.

[flash card]

> A card or other opaque material printed with words, numerals, or pictures and designed for rapid display.

This definition demonstrates that the intended use for media materials often dictates their medium designation. A set of flash cards all containing pictures would be assigned the GMD "flash card" and not the term "picture." The specific term given in 8.5B1. is the same as the GMD in this case, "flash card(s)" but, as with all specific designators, can be used in the singular or plural.

[game]

> A set of materials designed for play according to prescribed rules.

A definition as broad as this one allows the cataloger to assign this GMD to all types of nonprint media and some which might consist of only printed material. Description of print material would be taken from rules in Chapter 2, Books, Pamphlets, and Printed Sheets. Those items containing nonprint material, perhaps only graphics, would be described according to rules in Chapter 10.

The generic term "game" again can be applied to all types of games in the specific material designation, or the cataloger can choose a more specific word or phrase to accurately describe the type of game, such as "simulation game" or "simulation" according to 10.5B1. Although the nature of the play can be elaborated upon in the notes, an indication of the type of game is useful in this area.

[globe]

A model of a celestial body, usually the earth or the celestial sphere, depicted on the surface of a sphere.

The two types of globes are differentiated in the specific designation as either "globe" or "celestial globe" according to 3.5B1.

[kit]

An item containing two or more categories of material, no one of which is identifiable as the predominant constituent of the item; also designated multimedia kit (q.v.).

Additional information about the use of this GMD is given in *AACR 2* in a note accompanying the list of GMDs in 1.1C1. It explains that two types of formats are assigned this GMD, those in which the "relative predominance" of a part is not clear and those which are laboratory kits. If an item has a predominant component, such as a slide-tape presentation or a sound-filmstrip set, it is assigned the GMD appropriate for the part which carries the weight of the message. These examples would be cataloged as slides and filmstrips in most instances, because the message is contained in the visual component and the sound is meant as accompanying material to be used at the same time and with the visual. If the two items were to be used separately, they could fall within the definition of "kit" and would be assigned this GMD. All multipart items should not be assigned this designation, however. This will be a change for many libraries which have followed cataloging guidelines which made extensive use of the term "kit" to describe all multipart items.

It should be noted that the rules for the initial description of kits appear in Chapter 1, General Rules for Description under 1.10. ITEMS MADE UP OF SEVERAL TYPES OF MATERIALS. Because kits can contain formats of different types which are handled in several different chapters, they appear here. Three options are given for their physical description, and each option results in a different type of specific designator. The first option, 1.10C2. method a., suggests giving the extent of each group of items, such as 10 activity cards, 5 rulers, 5 thermometers, etc., followed by other information about the size of the package containing the items. This method is adequate only if no further description of the physical characteristics of the components is deemed necessary.

Because insufficient information is given to inform the user about characteristics which make necessary the use of different types of equipment, this method omits useful information for the library patron. More information can be given in the notes, however.

Method b. suggests giving a physical description on separate lines for each part or group of parts in the kit. In order to do this, the cataloger must then consult all of the chapters containing rules for each type of material described. The specific material designation for each part or each type of format is presented. For example, if a kit contains filmstrips and a film, the specific designators for the filmstrips would be chosen from the PHYSICAL DESCRIPTION AREA for filmstrips in rule 8.5. and from the list of specific designators in 8.5B1. The film would be described on a separate line with its own specific designator chosen from the rules for film, PHYSICAL DESCRIPTION AREA 7.5. and from the list of specific designators in 7.5B1.

Another method is given in the same rule. Method c. suggests that for packages with a large number of different types of material, a general term, "various pieces" with or without the total number of pieces can be used. This method obviously limits the use of the physical description and puts a great burden on the notes if any further information about the items in the package is to be a part of the catalog record.

[map]

> A representation, normally to scale and on a flat medium, of a selection of material or abstract features on, or in relation to, the surface of the earth or of another celestial body.

Many of the different types of maps are included in the list of suggested specific designators. Rule 3.5B1. lists 27 terms from which a choice can be made. This rule also allows for use of a more appropriate term if a specific designator from one of the other chapters covering nonprint materials is the more logical choice for its description. It would seem to be a better idea, however, to choose a term related to maps rather than one related to graphics for an item which, in the GMD, has been described as a map. If a map is a part of a more general graphic, the GMD [transparency] or [slide] or other GMD related to graphics summarized as graphics in the British list of GMDs might be applied to a map.

The rules seem to allow the cataloger to decide which is to be emphasized, the type of graphic in terms of its physical characteristics and use, or the type of a map which may be presented in several types of graphic formats, such as the transparency or slide. The choice of the GMD and the specific designator will determine the rest of the physical description. The choice should be made on the basis of the type of use of the material and the type of collection in which it is being cataloged. Libraries which have a separate map collection and use *AACR 2* will want to use Chapter 3; other libraries with omnimedia collections which integrate maps with other types of material may want to describe maps which are specific types of graphics according to Chapter 8.

[microform]

> A generic term for any medium, transparent, or opaque, bearing microimages.

According to *AACR 2*, all materials in a microformat, either an original publication or a publication originally published in another form and filmed, should be assigned the GMD [microform] and cataloged according to the rules in Chapter 11. See Chapter VIII of this text for the Library of Congress "rule interpretation" which stipulates that previously published books and serials will not be cataloged according to the rules for microforms. Specific material designations in 11.5B1. include:

aperture card(s)
microfiche(s) plus cassette if appropriate
microfilm(s) plus cartridge, cassette, or reel if appropriate
microopaque(s)

Optionally, the prefix "micro" can be dropped from the specific designation if used in the GMD. The Library of Congress will not follow the practice of dropping the prefix, which is probably preferable practice for most libraries.

[microscope slide]

A slide designed for holding a minute object to be viewed through a microscope or by a microprojector.

The reason that this type of slide is included in Chapter 10, rather than Chapter 8 which deals with photographic slides as graphic items, is implied in the definition. The microscope slide contains an object which in reality is three-dimensional. The same term is used in the specific designation, either in the singular or plural.

[model]

A three-dimensional representation of a real thing, either of the exact size of the original or to scale.

Only two specific terms are suggested, "mock-up" or "model." Another term may be chosen if appropriate, however. Again, additional information about a model can be given in notes, and in the case of models, this information might be included in a summary note.

[motion picture]

A length of film with or without recorded sound, bearing a sequence of images that create the illusion of movement when projected in rapid succession.

Several choices which cover the various containers for film are included in 7.5B1. They are:

film cartridge(s)   film loop(s)
film cassette(s)   film reel(s)

Optionally, the term "film" can be dropped from the specific designation when it is used in the GMD. However, its retention as the prefix aids the user in reading the physical description, and it probably should be retained.

[picture]

> A two-dimensional visual representation accessible to the naked eye and generally on an opaque backing.

This term is the most general GMD applied to graphics which do not fall into one of the other categories grouped according to the British graphic category. Specific designators which can be used with the GMD [picture] according to 8.5B1. include:

art reproduction(s)   poster(s)
photo(s)   radiograph(s)
picture(s)   stereograph(s)
postcard(s)   study print(s)

Other more specific terms may also be used with the GMD [picture]. These might include a term such as "stereograph reel." The most specific term applicable to all of the items in a package being cataloged should be used. In some instances, a package may contain several types of two-dimensional representations, and the term "picture" would be used as the specific designator as well as the GMD.

[realia]

> Actual objects (artifacts, specimens) as opposed to replicas.

Real items collected by a library can represent a broad range of different types of materials. Realia is the generic GMD to cover all of these materials. The specific designators should be chosen by the cataloger and should consist of a one or two word designator, descriptive of a single item or individual parts which comprise a group of real items cataloged together according to 10.5B1. An instructional package consisting only of realia and accompanied by printed material can be described as a kit or as realia with accompanying material. Most kits, however, contain other formats in addition to realia. If all of the objects in a multipart package are real objects, the general term can be used. A contents note or other type of note can give detail about the parts. The nature of real materials makes it impractical to attempt to record and use terms consistently in the specific material designation.

[slide]

> Transparent material on which there is a two-dimensional image, usually held in a mount, and designed for use in a projector or viewer.

Individual slides, sets of slides, and slides accompanied by sound or with integral sound are all assigned the GMD [slide]. They also are given the same specific designator "slide(s)" according to 8.5B1. Microscope slides are not included in this category.

[sound recording]

A recording on which sound vibrations have been registered by mechanical or electrical means so that the sound may be recorded.

Both musical and spoken word sound recordings are assigned this GMD. They are produced in several different formats and are found in current and archival collections. If the GMD is used, the cataloger may drop the term "sound" from the specific designator. Again, it is probably a better practice not to drop the term. Specific designators in 6.5B1. include:

sound cartridge(s)	sound tape reel(s)
sound cassette(s)	sound track film reel(s)
sound disc(s)	

Although the rule does not specifically state that the use of other terms can be applied, other terms could be used for types of material not covered in the list. Wire recordings are stored on spools, and piano and organ rolls could make use of the term "rolls."

[technical drawing]

A cross section, detail, diagram, elevation, perspective, plan, working plan, etc., made for use in an engineering or other technical context.

This GMD covers architectural renderings and other types of two-dimensional representations. The GMD and the specific designator are the same. Architectural models are cataloged as three-dimensional objects in Chapter 10.

[transparency]

A sheet of transparent material bearing an image and designed for use with an overhead projector or a light box. It may be mounted in a frame.

Materials produced for use with an overhead projector are categorized in this group. Although other photographic materials may be referred to as transparencies, they are not included here. Transparency masters on opaque material are not included and would be classified as pictures in the GMD with the optional term "master" used in the specific designation, "transparency master(s)." Transparencies will be assigned the same GMD and specific designator.

[videorecording]

A recording on which visual images, usually in motion and accompanied by sound, have been registered; designed for playback by means of a television set.

Specific types of videorecordings included in the specific designator according to 7.5B1. include:

videocartridge(s)	videodisc(s)
videocassette(s)	videoreel(s)

Optionally, the cataloger may drop the prefix "video" if it appears in the GMD. As with the term "film" in the specific designator "film reel(s)," dropping the prefix "video" in the specific designator is probably not a good idea. Retention of both will eliminate confusion on the part of the user of the cataloging record. Rule 7.5B1. suggests a variety of methods for cataloging several videorecordings of the same item, one using the term "videorecording" in the specific material designation and subsequently listing the various formats in which the item can be found in the collection. Another suggests using multilevel description found in Chapter 13, and the last is the use of a separate description for each item.

The final suggestion, a separate record for each item in the collection, is preferable from the user's point of view. With separate records, each item will be assigned the appropriate specific designation in the physical description area. The user will not have to interpret notes about availability in different formats. It is quite likely that a library will collect the same item in many different film and video formats. Consistency is easier to maintain with separate cataloging records than it is with multi-level description or use of notes to explain holdings.

Although the rule suggests that a more generic specific designator can be used when an item is available for purchase in several different video formats, this practice should be discouraged. The primary objective is to clearly and consistently catalog the library's holdings. To do this, each record should be used to uniquely identify an item in the collection and should use the most specific designator possible for the item in the specific designation. Because of incompatibility among videorecording systems and in some cases, film projection systems, information additional to that given in the specific material designation will often have to be given in the notes. Types of systems, not a specific manufacturer's name unless it is the only one to produce needed equipment, should be given when terms such as videocassette or film cartridge are used in the specific designator. In general, use the most specific term for the type of format for each item in the specific designator. Explain the type of system appropriate for the playback of the item in a note under Rule 7.7B10.(f).

1.1D.-1.1G. ELEMENTS FOLLOWING THE GMD

Rule 1.1E6. allows for the addition of an explanatory word or phrase as other title information, a rule which can be useful in indicating information about parts of a work selected for inclusion in a media presentation when a uniform title is not used. This is particularly true of sound recordings.

Statements of responsibility from the chief source(s) are recorded when they appear "prominently" in the item. Guidance in the interpretation of this term is given in the General Introduction Rule 0.8. which states that the information to which the term applies must be a formal statement found in one of the prescribed sources of information for Area 1. The cataloger must decide which individuals and groups are named prominently and record only those in this area. Others associated with the authorship, publication, production, etc. of the item can be named in one of several categories of notes. General notes related to responsibility appear in mnemonic rules .7B6. In some chapters, these rules include specific types of associated responsibility, such as cast and credits, for those not named in the statement of responsibility. If a statement of responsibility is not prominently presented and not needed for unique identification of the item, this information is given more clearly in the notes.

If a statement of responsibility is given, the phraseology found on the item will provide the most accurate indication of the relationship of those responsible to the item. Here again, there is often conflicting information in different sources related to nonprint. If possible, the chief source(s) should be used for this area. If the cataloger determines that several groups and individuals should be named, the order is determined by the order given in the chief source or can be given in the order which makes the most sense in terms of the way in which the item is produced or published according to 1.1F6. If the phraseology on the item does not make clear the relationship, the cataloger can add an explanatory word or phrase according to 1.1F8.

Because of possible differences in the choice of sources of information and because of differences in application of the rules which indicate that only prominently named groups and individuals be named in the statement of responsibility, cataloging records for some nonprint materials will differ from agency to agency. Large reference libraries may want to include more information in the body of the entry than will smaller libraries. Complete information about those responsible for nonprint items, whether given in the statement of responsibility or in the notes, will increase the usefulness of the cataloging records for many users. Previous rules have been criticized for not including coverage of information about those associated with responsibility for media materials. These rules allow for recording the information in several ways.

Many nonprint items contain collections of several different and sometimes diverse titles. Those lacking a collective title but having one part as a dominant part use the title of the dominant part as the title proper, with other parts named in notes according to 1.1G1. As is more often the case, items containing several titles lack a dominant part. Rule 1.1G2. says that:

> If, in an item lacking a collective title, no one part predominates, record the titles of the individually titled parts in the order in which they are named in the chief source of information, or in the order in which they appear in the item if there is no single chief source of information. Separate the titles of the parts by semicolons if the parts are all by the same person(s) or body (bodies), even if the titles are linked by a connecting word or phrase. If the individual parts are by different persons or bodies, or in the case of doubt, follow the title of each part by its parallel titles, other title information, and statements of responsibility and a full stop followed by two spaces.

Titles of individual parts are given with their parallel titles, other title information, and statements of responsibility for each part. The rule also outlines appropriate punctuation. Sound recordings, videorecordings, microforms, and other formats which can contain several titles can be handled under this rule.

1.2. EDITION AREA

The general rules applicable to all types of material in this section will, in most cases, also cover nonprint. Nonprint materials are not as often published in different editions as are print materials, but information about their edition and history of publication may be of interest to users. Items in nonprint formats are often reissued in the same or slightly different formats, reissued with a title change, repackaged with or without change of contents and title, or otherwise altered and presented as a new publication. In some instances, parts of a package are published as separate items and then collected to constitute a new offering. Edition statements found on the item seldom reflect these circumstances, however. When this information is given in a prescribed source of information, it can be given in the edition area. When it can be determined from other sources, it should be given in the notes area. Some specific rules relating to types of materials are found in the chapters dealing with nonprint. Particularly in the case of types of material easily edited, such as motion pictures and videorecordings, indication of the edited version in hand should be given as is indicated in the optional addition found in 7.2B3. If the statement cannot be given succinctly, it can be explained in a note as illustrated in 7.7B7. Information given in a note need not be from a prescribed source of information.

1.3. MATERIAL (OR TYPE OF PUBLICATION) SPECIFIC DETAILS AREA

No general rules for cartographic materials are given in Chapter 1. For cartographic materials and those which are published as serials, see Chapter 3 and Chapter 12.

1.4. PUBLICATION, DISTRIBUTION, ETC., AREA

According to Rule 1.4B1. "all information about the place, name, and date of all types of publishing, distribution, releasing and issuing activities" is to be given in this area. Because of the nature of contribution to the intellectual content by groups and individuals associated with the production of nonprint material, and because of the prominent way in which these are recorded in the bibliographic information appearing on nonprint material, catalogers may be inclined to name them in the statement of responsibility. This area, which provides a place in the body of the entry to name and designate the function of groups and individuals associated with publishing, etc., should be used, however. Publishers of nonprint materials are more closely related to content for nonprint than they are for print. This type of relationship is assumed by the users of the material and of the bibliographic entry. Names should be included in the statement of responsibility only when they go beyond the normal association of nonprint publisher. They are always recorded in this area with as much explanation about the relationship of the name to the item as the rules allow. Rule 1.4D3. allows for inclusion of a word or phrase found on the item explaining the relationship. Rule 1.4E. allows for the optional addition of a statement of function of a publisher, distributor, producer, and production company. The clarification provided by the application of this optional rule is desirable. The rule should be applied when the relationship is not otherwise made clear. If a publisher is named in the title or statement of responsibility, it must be repeated here, in shortened form if possible, according to 1.4D4.

Information about the manufacture of an item can also be included in this area according to 1.4B2. Although this rule suggests that a manufacturer can be named, the only circumstances under which the manufacturer is indicated is when the name of the publisher is unknown according to 1.4G1. If the cataloger is unsure whether an agency named is a manufacturer or publisher, the agency should be treated as a publisher according to 1.4D7. Also, 1.4E1. does not include an optional addition of the term "manufacturer" to the statement naming a publisher, distributor, etc. The use of the place, name, and date of manufacture is probably best reserved for catalog records of items containing no publication information, or for items which prominently provide information about manufacture which differs in place, name, and date from the place, name, or date of the publication of the item. The latter situation is covered in the optional rule 1.4G4.

1.4F.   DATE OF PUBLICATION, DISTRIBUTION, ETC.

In determining the date of publication of a nonprint item, the cataloger often must choose among dates given on several chief sources of information. In a single part item, refer to the source bearing a later date of publication and that part of the item which corresponds to the aspect in which the item is being treated. For example, for a study print with a copyright date for pictorial material and a later copyright date for instructional content, the cataloger would give the later date. That date represents the copyright of the item as a study print and not only as the previously copyrighted graphic. The date associated with the package as it is intended to be used is the date of copyright of the package.

Often multipart items bear several dates. The date chosen should be taken from a chief source, if possible, or from a unifying element for the package which indicates the copyright date of the publication of all of the parts as a package (see 1.0H.). Chapters covering types of nonprint formats also include rules for determining and transcribing dates associated with those specific types of media.

1.5.   PHYSICAL DESCRIPTION AREA

For nonprint materials, this area requires many detailed rules which appear in other chapters. Several general rules should be noted, however. Rules 1.5A3. and 1.7B16. provide an optional opportunity and directions for recording information about formats, other than the one in hand, in which the material is available. LC will apply the option, but for most libraries, this is probably not necessary and perhaps not a good idea. Unless the note makes perfectly clear the type of access for the various formats, whether available from the library or publisher, and gives a complete physical description of the formats, the information is of limited usefulness to the user. Also, information of this type can be confusing to the user of the bibliographic record because it does not directly relate to the item being described.

The rule covering the various ways in which accompanying material can be described, rule 1.5E., is important for nonprint materials. Four alternative methods are given. Any one agency may choose to use any one or all four. They include:

a.   make a separate entry in the catalog for each piece of material.

b.   use multilevel description found in Chapter 13.

c.   record details in a note.

d.   record the name of one or more types of accompanying materials at the end of the physical description for the one type of material being described as the dominant format.

An optional addition for method d. includes further physical description of each type of additional material based on rules for that type of format.

Method a. is probably not a good idea for many libraries. It adds many records to the catalog, provides separate entries for parts of an item intended to be used together, and fails to provide complete information on one record for a multipart item. Method b. may be used for some types of nonprint materials but is time-consuming, difficult to consistently apply, and confusing to the user. Method c. puts a heavy burden on the notes and omits basic information about the parts of a nonprint item from the physical description. If all of the information necessary for the use of the parts is worked into the notes, it may be a good choice, however.

Method d. allows for the inclusion of some information about all of the parts of a nonprint package and provides for optional expansion of basic information in the physical description. If the option is applied to any or all parts of a multipart item which is basically one type of format accompanied by a number of dependent parts, the description could become quite long and complicated. It should be remembered that this rule does not apply to kits, where parts are not dependent. The nature of accompanying material is that it is to be used with the predominant type of material contained in the package. Also, there are specific rules in the following chapters which more adequately cover certain types of multipart packages, such as games and realia found in Chapter 10.

1.6. SERIES AREA

A series, as it might apply to nonprint, is defined by the *AACR 2* Glossary as

> 1. A group of separate items related to one another by the fact that each item bears, in addition to its own title proper, a collective title applying to the group as a whole. The individual items may or may not be numbered ... (or) 3. A separately numbered sequence of volumes within a series or serial....

Single and multipart nonprint items containing parts of the same or different formats are published in series. These should be included in the description according to the rules for this area. Sets of materials also are often published as parts of series. A set of materials is a group of items published and packaged together, usually with a collective title; for example, four filmstrips with accompanying sound would constitute a set. That set may also be part of a series of sets, also with a collective series title. When cataloging a filmstrip set as a package rather than individual filmstrip titles, the series title and the numbering of that particular set within the series should be given. If individual filmstrips are cataloged separately, the set title and number, and the series title and number should be recorded as a series and subseries. In most instances, however, the set would be cataloged as one multipart item. Only the title for the series of sets with its number would be given in the series area.

A look at publishers' catalogs will reveal that some publishers list the same item as part of various pseudo-series, mainly for marketing purposes. Often, these pseudo-series lack collective titles and/or numbering and are listed as "related materials." These types of publishers' series are often too loosely related to be described in the series area.

1.7. NOTE AREA

Because information presented in the notes area need not be taken from one of the prescribed sources of information, much useful information about nonprint can be presented here when it cannot be given in the body of the entry, with or without brackets. Specific instructions about types and order of notes appear in Chapters 2-11 of *AACR 2*. Some general guidelines are given in Chapter 1. The use of quotations from the item, with an indication of the source, can clarify many issues of interest to the user. Also, formal notes, that is, those which are preceded by a consistently applied word or phrase, aid the user in understanding the categories of information presented in the notes. Their use should be considered by those who set policy for cataloging practice in a library. Some rules specify the introductory phrase used to precede certain information, such as cast and credits for films, found in Chapter 7. Contents and "with" notes are discussed in Chapter 1. One type of note where a consistently used phrase might be helpful is the note in 1.7B14., used to indicate intended audience. A library may choose to consistently use the phrase "Audience" preceding all types of information in this note. A school may choose to consistently apply grade level indications, age level indications, or other types of information in this note.

As mentioned above, notes relating to the statement of responsibility and to the area presenting information about publication, distribution, etc. can present relevant information not prominently found in the item in a prescribed source. Also, information related to the physical characteristics of the item can be expanded and explained in the notes.

1.8. STANDARD NUMBER AND TERMS OF AVAILABILITY AREA

Because most nonprint materials are not yet assigned standard numbers, as are books which carry the International Standard Book Number, rules in this area do not yet apply. Rule 1.8B3., however, instructs the cataloger to include any number which is useful in uniquely identifying the item in the notes under 1.7B19. In Chapter I, this note follows the contents note. For some types of materials, the publisher's number will appear in a different position. This is discussed in subsequent chapters. Rule 1.8D. provides for the optional addition of terms of availability. This can include information about price, availability through cooperating agencies, or rental availability and rental price. This area can be used to give information about nonprint items which are not necessarily part of the local collection, but can be made available through the collection.

1.10. ITEMS MADE UP OF SEVERAL TYPES OF MATERIAL

These rules which apply to multimedia kits and to items made up of one predominant format accompanied by another are of prime interest to nonprint catalogers. They appear in Chapter I because kits can be composed of numerous types of materials which may be covered in several of the chapters which follow in *AACR 2*. Rule 1.10B. reiterates the directions for treating an item with one predominant component: describe it first in the physical description, then either give the details of the accompanying material preceded by a plus, following the description of the predominant component in the physical description, or indicate only the extent of the accompanying material in the physical description, and give the details in a note. These rules are given in greater detail in 1.5E. for placement in the physical description and 1.7B11. for placement in the notes.

The rules for multimedia kits with two or more types of materials with no predominant component are in 1.10C. Items lacking a collective title are assigned GMDs appropriate to the type of material following each title proper. Few items will be handled in this way. The more common approach will be to use the GMD [kit] following a collective title, either on the item or supplied by the cataloger as instructed in rule 1.10C1. "Multimedia" is the term used by British catalogers and will not appear on North American catalog records. It should be remembered that when more specific rules are given in other chapters in *AACR 2*, such as those for multipart packages of realia or for games in Chapter 10, those rules are used rather than the general directions in Chapter 1.

Three methods can be used in describing multipart items made up of two or more formats. The first, 1.10C2a., is the least detailed, allowing for the enumeration of the types of parts. These terms can be taken from the specific designators from the chapters covering different types of nonprint materials or can be any other term which applies to the types of materials in the package. This method is only used if no further details about each of the types of nonprint are to be given in the physical description. The physical description using this method ends with the dimensions of the container of the package of materials. Notes can always be used to give additional information about the component parts.

The second method, 1.10C2b., is used when it is necessary to give additional details about the physical characteristics for the parts in the physical description. This method would be best used for nonprint component parts which would necessitate use of different types of equipment for one or more of the parts. The description for each part or type of parts is given on a separate line. To describe each type of material, rules from the chapters which apply to the type of materials are used. For example, a kit containing a filmstrip, a videotape, and a sound recording would be described in three physical descriptions, one using Chapter 8, one using Chapter 7, and one using Chapter 6. LC does not currently recommend use of this method.

The third method, 1.10C2c., is best used when a package contains a large number and variety of different types of materials, and when the parts do not necessitate use of different types of equipment. It simply designates the number of items in the package or indicates that the package contains an undetermined number of pieces which are assumed to be heterogeneous.

Notes on parts of multipart items can be given following the physical description as instructed in 1.10C3. This rule is inconsistent with the order of notes in chapters dealing with specific types or families of nonprint materials. It would be most appropriately used only with method a. or c. above. If separate physical descriptions are given for each of the types of component parts, notes relating to the physical description of each part should follow the order of notes for each separately described part, and those notes should relate to the order of types of materials in the physical description.

If parts of a multipart item are cataloged separately, rules for multilevel description found in Chapter 13 should be followed. In most cases, however, packages of multimedia material should be cataloged as a unit, and one of the above methods should be applied.

III
Description of Cartographic Materials

AACR 2 CHAPTER 3: CARTOGRAPHIC MATERIALS

3.0. GENERAL RULES

3.0A. SCOPE

The description of types of cartographic materials in this rule is fairly complete and gives examples of some of the many types of items which fall within the range of this chapter. Both two- and three-dimensional items which represent the earth or any other celestial body can be described with the rules in this chapter. Maps which are published in other formats, such as those covered in the graphics chapter like slides and transparencies, and those covered in other chapters such as the chapter on microforms, can also be described according to the rules in this chapter. Also, rules in several chapters can be combined to give complete description for an item which is a cartographic item, but by virtue of its format, can be assigned a GMD other than [map] or [globe] and can be described in the physical description as a slide, microform, transparency, etc.

In addition to the problems associated with material designation in dealing with cartographic materials, an international committee formed in 1979 known as the Anglo-American Cataloguing Committee for Cartographic Materials is addressing other issues. This group intends to publish a manual which should aid librarians by illustrating and clarifying some issues in this chapter and the *AACR 2* rules for entry in Chapter 21, which eliminates most corporate main entries for these materials. Map librarians generally prefer corporate entry and hope to persuade the major libraries, including the national libraries adopting *AACR 2*, to "interpret" rule 21.1B2. so that corporate entry for maps will be more common.

Developments with rules relating to these materials will be announced in various places including *LC Cataloging Service Bulletin* and *LC Information Bulletin*. Because of the unique and detailed nature of the materials themselves, a handbook such as the one previously mentioned and several aids used in working with maps which are listed at the end of this chapter should aid librarians who are attempting to interpret bibliographic information found on cartographic materials. These tools should also help in the application of the rules in their present form and in future "interpretations" of the rules in *AACR 2*.

The examples given at the end of this chapter will illustrate application of the rules as they are presently stated in the *AACR 2* text. They are presented as level 1 cataloging, with selective additional information. They represent the types of materials found in a general rather than special collection.

3.0B. SOURCES OF INFORMATION

Because atlases are book-like material, the sources of information for them is appropriately found in 2.0B.

3.0B2. Chief source of information

Two types of sources are permitted as the chief source for other cartographic items, the item(s) themselves and a container or attached unifying part. Unfortunately, there are no guidelines specific to cartographic materials given in *AACR 2* for determining which source to use when parts of an item with several chief sources yield conflicting or confusing information. The only guidance is found in 1.0H. which provides rules for single items and multipart items.

3.0B3. Prescribed sources of information

For each area, there are sources from which information can be taken without bracketing it. Examine the chief source(s) and extract information for the following areas:

Area 1. Title and statement of responsibility
2. Edition
3. Mathematical data
4. Publication, distribution, etc.
6. Series

If not found there, examine accompanying printed material and extract information for the following areas:

Area 2. Edition
3. Mathematical data
4. Publication, distribution, etc.
6. Series

Take from any source, information for areas:

Area 5. Physical description
7. Notes
8. Standard number and terms of availability.

3.0D. LEVELS OF DETAIL IN THE DESCRIPTION

Perhaps recognizing that many multimedia libraries may have small collections of maps which, because of the nature of their use and the limited needs of the patrons in terms of bibliographic description, the choice of level of description for maps may differ from the choice of level for other types of nonprint and print publications. In this text, level 2 is the basic level suggested with the selective addition of certain types of information not mandated in level 2. Many libraries may want to adopt level 1 for maps and selectively add information according to their needs. The first element in Area 3.3. MATHEMATICAL DATE AREA, the scale of the item, is to be included even when using only level 1. All of the elements in 3.3. are to be used when using level 2 or level 3.

3.0J.   DESCRIPTION OF WHOLE OR PART

Even when a group of maps has a collective title, three options are given for the description of the whole group or of the parts. The first is description of the collection as a whole. If this option is chosen, generous use of notes describing the parts is necessary. The second option is to make a separate description of each separate map. If this is done, the set of maps becomes a series, and the collective title either given on the items or supplied becomes the series title. The third option is to use multilevel description. Although this type of description has not been recommended for other types of nonprint materials, this option may provide the best type of description for cartographic materials. If this option is chosen, the cataloger follows the rules in this chapter and in Chapter 13.

Multilevel description allows for basic description both of the collection as a whole and individual items within the collection. Because of the amount of detail required to adequately describe maps, this option which allows for fairly complete descriptions of both units is placed in the cataloging record in such a way that each part is described before the various notes relating to the individual part are given. Multilevel description clarifies for the user what the separate unit belongs to and the nature of the separate part and of the collection.

Depending upon the nature of the items being cataloged, any cataloging agency may want to use all of the different methods. There is no need to exclusively use one optional method. Also, it should be remembered that level 1, 2, or 3 can be used with any of these methods.

3.1.   TITLE AND STATEMENT OF RESPONSIBILITY AREA

Title information is recorded as instructed in 1.1.

3.1C.   OPTIONAL ADDITION. GENERAL MATERIAL DESIGNATION

Although the Library of Congress will not use a GMD for cartographic materials, other libraries integrating cataloging records for these materials with other print and nonprint items will probably want to do so.

3.1F.   STATEMENTS OF RESPONSIBILITY

Individual cartographers and individuals named on the item who are associated with a facet of responsibility, such as an editor, are given in this area. Organizations and corporate names are given here only if responsibility is attributed to them. If this is not clear from the item, these names may only appear in the publication area. Names related to responsibility, either not appearing prominently in the chief source or not considered important to the unique identification of the item, can be put in notes under 3.7B6.

3.1G.   ITEMS WITHOUT A COLLECTIVE TITLE

A collection of cartographic items without a collective title can be described as a unit or described separately for each individually titled part. Although not mentioned in this section of the rules, an item for which a collective title is supplied can be described in multi-level description like a titled collection.

3.1G2.

Recording individual titles of parts, as instructed in 1.1G. for collections lacking a title but described as a unit, produces a title and statement of responsibility area which is very confusing to the user. It also complicates other areas of the description.

3.1G4.

Making a separate description for parts, particularly where the parts are not related in content and a collective title is inappropriate, is an alternative approach to cataloging an untitled collection as a unit. Care must be taken in constructing the physical description of each part, and the separate descriptions must be linked with a note according to 3.7B21.

3.2. EDITION AREA

Record edition statements as instructed in 1.2. The optional addition of an edition statement which is not found on the item will not be done by LC. Such information will be given in a note.

3.3. MATHEMATICAL DATA AREA

English is used in this area, regardless of the language of the rest of the description.

3.3B. STATEMENT OF SCALE

This element is always included for cartographic material. If found on the item, it is given as a ratio without brackets. If it must be calculated from the verbal scale or if it is found in a source other than the chief source, then it is bracketed. If it is calculated from other information on the item the abbreviation "ca." should precede the information.

3.3B2. Optional addition.

LC will add additional scale information found on the item. Because this type of information is more easily understood by the nonspecialist than the ratio information which must be given, the addition would be a welcome one for most library users, even in those libraries choosing to use level 1. For methods used to calculate scales for these materials, see the aids at the end of the chapter.

3.3C. STATEMENT OF PROJECTION

For level 2 or 3, give this statement according to 3.3C1. LC will add the optional associated phrases related to projection as instructed in 3.3C2. Rather than add the statement of coordinates and equinox in 3.3D., LC will give other meridians found on the item in the notes area.

3.4. PUBLICATION, DISTRIBUTION, ETC., AREA

The directions for this area found in 1.4. are followed for cartographic materials. LC will exercise the option to add the name of the distributor as well as the publisher as instructed in 3.4D1. They will add a statement of function as instructed in 3.4E1. only for clarification. The date is recorded as instructed in 1.4F. The optional addition of information about printing given in 3.4G2. will be added by LC only if it is very important to the item.

3.5. PHYSICAL DESCRIPTION AREA

The terms given as specific designators in 3.5B1. can be found in most general dictionaries and are better explained in reference tools related to cartographic materials. If a map published in another format is cataloged according to the rules in this chapter and is assigned the GMD [map], it can . nevertheless be assigned a specific designator, such as flip chart, wall chart, slide, transparency, microfiche, etc. from the terms listed as specific designators in the appropriate chapter (usually Chapter 8 Graphic Materials). Other physical details for atlases include the number of maps in the atlas; for maps, etc., they include color, material, and mounting. Rules for determining dimension given in 3.5D. are quite detailed. LC will add the optional dimension for depth of a relief model as instructed in 3.5D3. They will also add the optional dimensions of a container as instructed in 3.5D5.

3.5E.   ACCOMPANYING MATERIAL
The name and the physical description of accompanying material, particularly any which requires equipment for use, should be given at the end of the physical description.

3.7.   NOTE AREA
Much information can be given in the note area, particularly when using level 1 for cartographic materials in a collection which has relatively few such materials, and does not describe the materials for the specialized user but for the generalist.

3.7B1.   Nature and scope of the item
This type of note can relate to various aspects of the material but should not include information related to its physical characteristics. This information is better given in 3.7B10. and should not be given here if a contents note would be more complete and cover the information more fully. Scope is often covered in other parts of the description, including the title, titles of contents, and contents notes, in general.

3.7B3,4,5.
Title notes are often needed because several titles appear in various places and in different forms on cartographic materials. The notes aid in the unique identification of the items.

3.7B6.   Statements of responsibility
Many individuals and groups may be named on cartographic material, and when few are chosen for the statement of responsibility area in the body of the entry, others should be named here. Their relationship with the material should be made clear. They can be grouped in one note or given in individual notes.

3.7B7.   Edition and history
These materials often provide such information on the item itself, because it is significant to the content. Liberal use should be made of these types of notes.

3.7B8.   Mathematical and other cartographic data
These notes can provide data which is supplementary to the information required in area 3.3. When level 1 is used and only the scale is given in the body as a ratio, the other information omitted from this area in the body can be given in the note area if deemed important or useful.

3.7B9. Publication, distribution, etc.

Information which is omitted from this area in the body and not included in the edition and history note can be included here.

3.7B11. Accompanying material

Notes explaining noncartographic material should be given here. If separate entries or multilevel description are not used for collections, this note and the contents note carry the burden of description for parts of a collection. If parts of a collection differ significantly, it may be necessary to give detailed information for each part.

3.7B18. Contents

When collections are described as a unit, this note must provide information about all of the parts. The difficulty of giving enough information in this note is demonstrated by the instructions and examples in this rule. Items with a collective title, with some unity of contents, can adequately be covered. However, collections of diverse materials pose a problem and are better cataloged separately or with multilevel description.

3.7B21. "With" notes

When separately titled parts of a collection are given separate descriptions, this note is needed to bring the materials together.

EXAMPLES:
Descriptive Cataloging for Cartographic Materials

Hammond large type world atlas [map]. — Scales vary. —
Maplewood, N.J. : Hammond, 1979.

1 atlas (144 p.) : 51 col. maps ; 32 cm.

Intended audience: Visually handicapped.

ISBN 0-8437-1246-5.

Atlases are described like book material with the addition of the scale in the body and some variation in the physical description to indicate the map content of the item.

———————

Generalized geologic map of Tennessee [map] / State of Tennessee
Department of Conservation, Division of Geology. — Scale
1:3,168,000. — [Nashville, Tenn.] : The Department, 1970.

1 map : col. ; 22 x 28 cm.

Robert E. Hershey, director and state geologist.

Entry under title rather than group responsible. Scale given for level 1. Note relates to statement of responsibility.

———————

Forest, J.
   France [map] : agriculture, industrie, et commerce / par
J. Forest. − Scale 1:1,200,000. − Paris : Girard et
Barrere, [196-] (Paris : Imprimeries Michard, 1966)

   1 map : col. ; 93 x 120 cm.

   Text in French.

   Depot legal no. 590.

      I. Title.

Language of the description is that of the item. Entry under cartographer named
on the item. Optional addition of information about printer. Number given on
the item.

Chequamegon National Forest, Hayward, Washburn, Glidden
   Ranger Districts [map] : Wisconsin fourth principal
   meridian / U. S. Department of Agriculture, Forest
   Service. − Scale 1:126,720 ; Polyconic proj. 1927 North
   American Datum. − [Washington] : The Department :
   U.S. Government Printing Office [distributor], 1977.

   1 map : col. ; 111 x 75 cm.

   Compiled at the Regional Office, Milwaukee, Wisconsin,
1966 from U.S. Geological Survey quadrangles.

   Updated revisions made from 1976 U.S. Forest Service
Township maps and the latest U.S. Geological Survey
quadrangles.

   GPO no.: 1978-753 463.

      I. United States. Forest Service.

Title proper contains punctuation altered to simplify what is on the source. Other
title information explains title proper. Statement of responsibility on item. Both
scale and projection taken from item. Shortened form of the name of the
publisher already given in the statement of responsibility. U.S. GPO is not
publisher but only distributor as indicated in optional statement of function.

(Examples continue on page 64)

Tsopelas, D.
  Road map of Greece [map] / D. Tsopelas, cartographer. —
Scale 1:1,230,000. — Athens : National Tourist Organization of
Greece, 1972.

  1 map : col. ; 62 x 74 cm. folded to 22 x 12 cm.

  Place names in Greek, legend in English.
  Title on outside of folded map: Map of Greece.
  Inset on front: Map of communications in Greece.
  On verso: Maps of 6 regions. Scale 1:500,000.

    I. Title.

Entry under cartographer prominently named on item. Scale given on item.
Language notes. Title proper from map and other title given in note. Insert map
noted. Regional maps with different scale included in note only because of
relative importance to general map.

  1979 highway map of Arkansas [map] / prepared and issued
    by the Arkansas State Highway and Transportation Depart-
    ment, Division of Planning and Research. —
    Scale 1:316,800. — Little Rock, Ark. : The Department,
    [197-]

  1 map : col. ; 53 x 58 cm. on sheet 56 x 81 cm. folded
to 19 x 14 cm.

  On verso: Enlargements of 16 major cities and Interstate
Highways 30, 40, and 55.

  Indicates public recreation areas.
  Includes state mileage chart.

    I. Arkansas. State Highway and Transportation Dept.

Title recorded as appears on the item, including date. Statement of responsibility
on the item and scale. Decade certain. Size of main map given because it differs
significantly from sheet size. Notes related to intended use of map.

The World [map] / prepared and published under the direction of the Department of Defense. — 1st ed. — Scale 1:11,000,000. — [Washington, D.C.] : U.S. Army Naval Oceanographic Office, [1970]

9 maps : col. ; 95 x 130 cm.

Scale: 1 in. = 174 statute miles at the equator ; Mercator projection.
Relief shown by gradient tints, shading, and spot heights.

A collection of maps with a collective title on the item. Edition statement on the item. Scale given in body of entry with optional scale information put in notes. Projection in notes because entry is level 1 with a few additions, such as place and expanded physical description. It should be remembered that level 1 indicates a minimum of required elements. The cataloger can add selectively other useful information.

AIDS FOR CATALOGING
CARTOGRAPHIC MATERIALS

Map Scale Indicator (a device for calculating scales) available from Continental Cartographics, P.O. Box 2704, Madison, WI 53701.

American Geographical Society. *Cataloging and Filing Rules for Maps and Atlases in the Society's Collections.* New York, NY: The Society, 1969.

Boggs, Samuel W., and Dorothy C. Lewis. *The Classification and Cataloging of Maps and Atlases.* New York, NY: Special Libraries Association, 1945.

Bonacker, Wilhelm. *Kartenmacher Aller Länder Und Zeiten.* Stuttgart: Anton Hiersemann, 1966.

Library of Congress Catalog: Maps and Atlases, 1953-55. (See any recent LC Catalog for availability.)

Moore, Barbara N. *A Manual of AACR 2 Examples for Cartographic Materials.* Lake Crystal, MN: Soldier Creek Press, 1981.

Tooley, Ronald. *Tooley's Dictionary of Mapmakers.* New York, NY: Alan R. Uss, Inc., 1979. (pre-1900 cartographers).

IV
Description of Sound Recordings

AACR 2 CHAPTER 6: SOUND RECORDINGS

6.0. GENERAL RULES

6.0A. SCOPE
This chapter covers sound discs, tapes, rolls, and film on which only sound is recorded. It can be used for various types of archival recordings, such as those on wire, with some improvisation in the elements of the physical description.

Because of the nature of the types of materials found on sound recordings, several other sections of *AACR 2* need to be considered in bibliographic description of these formats. Spoken word, musical, and recordings which are a mixture of the two often require or can be assigned uniform titles. A uniform title as defined by *AACR 2* is:

> The particular title by which a work that has appeared under varying titles is to be identified for cataloguing purposes. A conventional collective title used to collate publications of an author, composer, or corporate body containing several works or extracts, etc., from several works, e.g., complete works, several works in a particular literary or musical form.

Uniform titles are used to bring together in the catalog all of the varying forms of an item, and the title proper with the other elements of description provides unique identification of the item. The uniform title aids in access, particularly in cases where the title proper does not give sufficient information for identification or where the title by which an item is known differs from the title proper. They can be used for both spoken word and musical sound recordings. Rules for application and formation of uniform titles appear in Chapter 25. The decision to apply a uniform title is based on several considerations outlined in 25.1. In deciding to use uniform titles, the weight given to these considerations is decided by each agency. As the sharing of resources between libraries of different types increases, a consistent policy of application of uniform titles can certainly aid in access to recorded sound materials by all types of library patrons. Even in a small collection, the use of uniform titles is becoming more important for identification.

According to 25.2A., the uniform title is enclosed in square brackets and given before the title proper. If given as the main entry heading, the uniform title can optionally be given without brackets, as the Library of Congress has chosen to do. When a uniform title is used as main entry, access is still provided for the title proper. When entry is under another heading, access is provided by an added entry both under the title proper and name-title entry(s) under variant forms of the title.

Most sound recordings to which uniform titles are applied are musical and are covered in the basic rules in Chapter 25 dealing with individual and collective titles, rules 25.1.-25.12. and in rules 25.25.-25.36., which relate specifically to music.

As previously discussed, the rules in Part I do not deal with entry, choice of access points provided in added entries, or with form of entries. Rules for headings, uniform titles, and references or added entries for all types of material, both print and nonprint, appear in Part II. Because of their unique nature, sound recordings are treated separately from other materials in 21.23. For a discussion of points presented in the rules for entry for sound recordings, see Chapter IX, "Access Points for Nonprint" in this text.

Examples included at the end of this chapter will illustrate application of these rules.

6.0B. SOURCES OF INFORMATION

6.0B1. Chief source of information
The chief source of information which is the preferred source for most areas is the label affixed permanently to the item itself and an integral container label for those formats which have such containers, such as the cassette and cartridge case. In the case of multipart items, all of the labels for each of the parts are considered to be the chief source for the item. Other material, if it is the only source of a collective title, is considered to be the chief source. When information is not available from the chief source, it can be taken from:

accompanying material
a container which is not integral
other sources.

Unlike other formats, information presented in the recording itself is not preferred over the information found in text on labels.

6.0B2. Prescribed sources of information
For each area, there are prescribed source(s) from which information can be taken without bracketing it in the description. Examine the chief source(s) and extract information for the following areas:

Area 1. Title and statement of responsibility
2. Edition
4. Publication, distribution, etc.
6. Series

Next examine the accompanying textual material and extract information for:

Area 2.   Edition
     4.   Publication, distribution, etc.
     6.   Series

If information for these three areas is not in either the chief source or the accompanying material, look for it on a container which is not integral.

Take from any source information for the remaining areas:

Area 5.   Physical description
     7.   Notes
     8.   Standard number and terms of availability

6.1.   TITLE AND STATEMENT OF RESPONSIBILITY AREA

6.1B.   TITLE PROPER

Determining the extent of the title proper is important because of the placement of the GMD immediately after it and preceding the other title information and parallel titles. Spoken word recordings are covered in the rule in 1.1B. Alternative titles and names of composers or others that are an integral part of the title are considered part of the title proper. A long title can be abridged according to 1.1B4.

Title proper for musical sound recordings is determined according to 6.1B., 1.1B., and 5.1B2. Musical titles can be distinctive titles unrelated to the type of composition or production, or can be titles descriptive of the type of composition, consisting of a generic term such as "symphony," "quartets," "choral," and other distinguishing descriptive elements such as the medium of performance, if not implied in the generic term, the key, and various numbers associated with the composition. If the title proper consists of a generic term in combination with other descriptive elements, all of this information is considered to be part of the title proper. All of the elements are needed in the title proper to uniquely identify the title. This is not supplementary information, such as that presented in other title and parallel title information.

Often, all of the information in the title proper will also be used in the uniform title. The difference is in the order of the elements which determine filing in the catalog. The uniform title uniquely identifies the composition; the title proper helps to uniquely identify the item being cataloged. Both are necessary. According to rule 1.1B1., the title proper should be recorded from the prescribed source of information on the item exactly as it appears in terms of wording, order, and spelling. Punctuation and capitalization of the title on the item can be changed. This is often necessary and desirable in the cataloging record because punctuation on the item is often insufficient and the layout makes punctuation unnecessary. Also, the type used on the item for recording titles does not indicate appropriate capitalization.

In the case of an item for which the cataloger must supply a title according to 1.1B7., the cataloger has help in devising the title. The rules for uniform titles for musical compositions instruct the cataloger as to the elements and their order for constructing a title proper. A supplied title may also be taken from a source other than the prescribed sources and must be bracketed. The source of the title is indicated in the note area. Some examples follow:

Title proper

> Don Juan ballettmusik
>
> Sonate pour violon et piano en la majeur
>
> L'elistir d'amore-highlights
>
> Sinfonias op. 6, 8, 9.
>
> Also sprach Karl Farkas
>
> Music for solo flute
>
> Quartet in G minor for piano and strings,
>   K. 478
>
> The six viola quintets
>
> Concerto for violin and orchestra in B minor, op. 61
>
> [Germelshausen]
>   note: Title from narration.

6.1C. OPTIONAL ADDITION. GENERAL MATERIAL DESIGNATION

Immediately after the title proper, the GMD [sound recording] is given:

GMD added

> The starlight express [sound recording] : incidental music, op. 78
>
> Electronic pioneers [sound recording]
>
> Dance service II [sound recording]
>
> Symphony no. 3 in E flat major (eroica) op. 55
>   [sound recording]
>
> Die Walküre : ride of the Valkyries ; Tristan und
> Isolde : prelude to Act 1 ; Götterdämmerung : Siegfried's funeral
> music ; Siegfried : forest murmurs [sound recording] /
> Richard Wagner. —

Rule 25.5E. instructs the cataloger to use the GMD in the uniform title beginning with an upper case letter and enclosed in the same brackets used for the uniform title. The Library of Congress has decided not to apply this rule and will show the GMD in its own brackets, beginning with a lower case letter following the title proper only. It would probably be wise for most libraries to follow this example for reasons of consistency with the general rules for GMDs in 1.1C1. and for filing purposes.

6.1D. PARALLEL TITLES

Musical sound recordings often are published with titles in several languages, usually with the title proper given in either the language of the original composition or the language of the market in which the publisher expects the largest sales. The uniform title is formulated preferably using the composer's original language and optionally, a better known title in another language according to rule 25.27A. The title proper, however, is the first title or the most prominent title in the chief source of information for the item. Parallel titles which should be recorded are all those titles in other languages also appearing in the chief source:

Parallel titles

La fille du regiment [sound recording] = The daughter of the regiment

Les amants turcs [sound recording] = I traci amanti

Highlights from Le nozze di Figaro [sound recording] = The marriage of Figaro

6.1E. OTHER TITLE INFORMATION

Both musical and spoken word recordings often have other title information which augments the title proper, usually with a descriptive phrase. Rules in 1.1E. apply to sound recordings. Lengthy information can be abridged according to 1.1E3. Other title information related to parallel titles can be optionally added to the title to which it applies, according to 1.1E5. A bracketed, supplied addition to the title explaining the title proper can be added as other title information according to 1.1E6, but this information can be better covered in a summary or contents note:

Other title information

Social orchestra [sound recording] : a collection of popular melodies: published in 1854

Developments in civil procedure, 1979 [sound record-ing] : a one-hour discussion

Zarzuela [sound recording] : Jose Carreras sings Spanish arias

6.1F. STATEMENTS OF RESPONSIBILITY

Names of those responsible for the intellectual or musical content, not those responsible for the performance or production of the material, are given in this area. Only when the performance constitutes the creation of the recorded material are performers mentioned in the statement of responsibility. This can be the case with unique performances of contemporary music where the performance constitutes the event which is recorded. If the contents can be performed in the same way, at another time, by the same or different performers, the performers should not be recorded here. Performers are important for description, however, and should be described in notes.

A word or phrase explaining the nature of the responsibility of persons or groups named can be added, in brackets, to the statement of responsibility according to 6.1F3. If a phrase appears on the chief source, it can be taken from that source and added without brackets.

Statement of responsibility

Contours for orchestra [sound recording] / Hale Smith. —

Annie [sound recording] : a new Broadway musical / lyrics
by Martin Charnin ; music by Charles Strouse ; book by
Thomas Meehan. —

Diverse ayres on sundrie notions [sound recording] /
(S. 99 44/100) : for bargain counter tenor and keyboard / P.D.Q.
Bach ; cunningly transcribed by Peter Schickele. —

Creativity [sound recording] : reflections and remina-
tions / [lecture by] Winston Weathers. —

Address to the U.S. Congress, 1941 [sound recording] /
Winston Churchill. —

Goodbye, Columbus [sound recording] : music from the
sound track of the motion picture featuring songs / composed
and performed by The Association. —

Close encounters of the third kind [sound recording] : original
soundtrack / composed by Johnny Williams. —

6.1G.   ITEMS WITHOUT A COLLECTIVE TITLE

Sound recordings, particularly those with musical content, commonly
contain diverse works for which a collective title is inappropriate and not given.
The cataloger needs to be concerned with adequate description and access for all
of the parts. Items of this type can be described either as a unit or as separate
parts. Adequate access is possible, in either case, if the cataloging agency does not
limit the number of access points for each bibliographic record. Cataloging
records for these items described as a unit are more complicated and may not be
as clear to the user. Usually, they do require fewer cards in a card catalog and
fewer records in an automated catalog, however. Items described separately
present fewer problems for the cataloger and may make access easier for the user.
They do add to the total number of records in the catalog, however.

Although some nonprint materials, particularly those which are
educationally oriented, are best handled as units published, users of sound
recordings are usually interested in an individual title rather than in the collective
unit. Coupled with increased ease in the application of the rules for description,
this factor may help the cataloging agency make decisions about the way in which
all such items will be handled or the way in which each item should be considered
on an individual basis. In any case, the agency should consider the options
provided by the rules and try to consistently apply a policy decision. LC has
chosen to catalog items without a collective title under one entry consisting of all
of the titles on the item, whereas it formerly used several entries connected by
"with" notes. This is another consideration for individual libraries making a
decision about this issue. Consult 6.1G. and 1.1G. to record the titles, and 1.1C.,
particularly 1.1C2. for placement of the GMD.

6.1G1.

This rule indicates the two ways an item lacking a collective title can be
described, either individually or as one unit. LC will describe these as a unit.

6.1G2.

Titles for collections lacking a collective title are recorded according to 1.1G.
Although the first rule in this section 1.1G1. indicates that a predominant part of

an item lacking a collective title can be used as the title proper with other parts named in a contents note, this approach is inadequate for sound recordings. A part may seem predominant by virtue of its duration in relation to other parts, but information about minor parts may be important for the user and cannot be described in enough detail in only a contents note. Recording all of the titles in the body of the entry often produces a long title statement. It does, however, more closely match the bibliographic information on the item than do the other methods.

6.1G2.

Items described as a unit are covered in this rule which the cataloger should note was incorrectly printed in the rules. The correct version, is as follows:

> If, in an item lacking a collective title, no one part predominates, record the titles of the individually titled parts in the order in which they are named in the chief source of information, or in the order in which they appear in the item if there is no single chief source of information. Separate the titles of the parts by semicolons if the parts are all by the same person(s) or body (bodies), even if the titles are linked by a connecting word or phrase. If the individual parts are by different persons or bodies, or in the case of doubt, follow the title of each part by its parallel titles, other title information, and statements of responsibility and a full stop followed by two spaces.

Recording the title proper in this manner can produce a very complicated record.

Items without a collective title described as a unit

Die Walküre : ride of the Valkyries ; Tristan und Isolde : prelude to Act I ; Götterdämmerung : Siegfried's funeral music ; Siegfried : forest murmurs [sound recording] / Richard Wagner. —

Quartet in G minor for piano and strings, K. 478 ; Quintet in E-flat for piano and winds, K. 452 [sound recording] / Mozart

Rhapsody in blue ; An American in Paris [sound recording] / George Gershwin. —

6.1G4.

Instead of recording all of the titles in a collection which lacks a collective title, the cataloging agency may choose to provide a separate entry for each titled part. If this rule is followed, care must be taken to provide a physical description which relates to the separate part being cataloged according to 6.5B3. The descriptions for each separate part are linked together with a note according to 6.7B21.

Items without a collective title described as separate parts

Die Walküre [sound recording] : ride of the Valkyries / Richard Wagner. —

Tristan und Isolde [sound recording] : prelude to Act
I / Richard Wagner. —

Quartet in G minor for piano and strings, K. 478
[sound recording] / Mozart. —

Rhapsody in blue [sound recording] / George
Gershwin. —

1.1G4.
Going back to Chapter 1 of *AACR 2*, the cataloger is given the option of
using the one predominant title as the title proper according to 1.1G1. This is not
recommended. Another method is to choose several predominant parts for the
title statement and list the others in a note according to 1.1G4.

Application of this rule, which again suggests use of only a contents note for
the title of a unique part, is not recommended.

6.2. EDITION AREA

Information concerning the edition of a sound recording can be taken from
the item, accompanying material, or a container without adding brackets. It
should be recorded as instructed in 1.2B. The Library of Congress will not apply
the optional addition of an edition statement for an item which does not contain
that information in one of the prescribed places. This information can be given in
a note under 6.7B7. For items without a collective title described as a unit, edition
statements can be given for parts. This complication also demonstrates the
advisability of describing such materials in separate entries.

6.4. PUBLICATION, DISTRIBUTION, ETC., AREA

6.4C. PLACE OF PUBLICATION, DISTRIBUTION, ETC.
As instructed in 1.4C., the cataloger should record a place of publication,
preferably one taken from the item, accompanying material, or the container. If
the information is not available there, reference sources should be consulted.
Reference sources listed in the bibliography of cataloging aids, Appendix I, and
bibliography of selected nonprint bibliographies and directories, Appendix V, at
the end of this text should provide this information.

Care should be taken to determine the place of the publisher, distributor,
and of the particular subdivision of a parent organization with tools which give
information about the item as it was originally published. If it is determined
through reference sources that the place, publisher, and/or distributor for the
item have changed, this information can be given in a note, perhaps concerning
current availability. In the description, the item in hand as it was originally
published is the information to be given in the body of the description.
Conjectural information should be followed by a question mark within brackets,
as instructed in 1.4C6.

6.4D. NAME OF PUBLISHER, DISTRIBUTOR, ETC.
The names of both the publisher and distributor should be recorded
according to 1.4D. Although optional, the name of the distributor is important
for sound recordings, and LC has chosen to exercise this option. It is
recommended that other libraries should also follow this practice. The

subdivision of a company associated with the publication should be used rather than the name of a parent organization. It should be a functional organization rather than a series under which a number of recordings have been issued by a company. Such a statement should appear as a series statement. Most such statements will not be numbered but, nevertheless, constitute a series for sound recordings, a concept somewhat different from a series for other materials. It is sometimes difficult to differentiate between a series and a trade name or brand name of a publisher. The catalog of the publisher or a reference source for sound recordings can help to clarify the facts of publication.

6.4E. OPTIONAL ADDITION. STATEMENT OF FUNCTION OF PUBLISHER, DISTRIBUTOR, ETC.

Because several names may be given in this area, this optional addition can help to clarify the information for the user and should be used in cases where the functions are not clear. LC will apply this option, but not necessarily uniformly. For major companies, it may not be necessary, but for less well known organizations, it can be helpful for the user.

6.4F. DATE OF PUBLICATION, DISTRIBUTION, ETC.

Several dates associated with the performance, recording, pressing, and copyright of the publication may appear in one or several of the sources of information. The new copyright law, the inconsistent and misleading way in which publishers of many materials, including sound recordings, give dates and copyright notices on materials, and the inability of the cataloger to determine accurate information about copyright date has led the Library of Congress to a tentative decision to provide information about publication date while omitting the date of copyright. See LC *Cataloging Service Bulletin*, No. 10, pp. 15-16 and *Cataloging Service Bulletin*, No. 11, p. 18 for more information. In most cases, the latest date on the item represents the publication date for the item in hand. Information concerning date of recording, copyright of accompanying textual material, etc. can be given in a note as directed in 6.7B7. if it is important. The symbol p. enclosed in a circle represents the date of copyright for sound material. If a copyright date is given and the symbol is used, it should be changed to c. . The date is given as information about the fact of copyright, rather than as a transcription of the actual information as it appears on the item.

6.4G. PLACE OF MANUFACTURE, NAME OF MANUFACTURE, DATE OF MANUFACTURE

If information about the publisher is unknown, and information about manufacture is available, this information is given. LC will apply the option to provide this information in addition to publication information on a selective basis. For major companies it is probably not necessary, but for smaller companies it should be given.

Publication, distribution, etc., area

Norwalk, Conn. : Cook Laboratories, c1976.

Tulsa, Okla. : J. Nickols, c1978.

Santa Barbara, Calif. : Center for the Study of Democratic Institutions, [1976]

New York : Audio Fidelity, 1959.

New York : Caedmon Records, 1973.

[London] : Angel, 1968.

[New York] : RCA Victor, 1962.

New York : Sesame Street Records : Manufactured and distributed by Distinguished Productions, 1978.

Berkeley, Calif. : Pacifica Archive, 1968.

Deland, Fla. : Everett Edwards, c1972.

North Hollywood, Calif. : Bowman, [196-?]

Santa Monica, Calif. : BFA Educational Media ; [New York : Holt Information Systems, distributor, 1972]

[New York] : RCA Red Seal, 1978.

Hollywood, Calif. : Discreet, 1974 ([New York] : Warner Bros. Records)

New Rochelle, N.Y. : Spoken Arts, 1956.

Brooklyn, N.Y. : Produced and distributed by 3R Sound, 1972.

6.5. PHYSICAL DESCRIPTION AREA

Sound recording formats

There are two major types of sound recordings at present, sound recorded magnetically on tape, or sound pressed into discs. Sound tape is described in terms of the type of integral container — cartridge, cassette, or reel. Again, the cartridge contains a continuous loop and the cassette contains two reels with the tape transported across the playing head in both directions. All magnetic tape is only recorded on one side. Although often marked as side one or side two, the actual recording of both sides is on different parts of the same side of the tape. To replay the first track, side one of the container will face upward on the machine. To replay track two, side two of the container will face upward. Reel-to-reel tape is played in only one direction for full-track tape, but is played in two directions for two- or four-track tape.

There are several types of materials used as the base for blank tape which is to be recorded magnetically. The tape itself is all similar and can be recorded in a number of different track configurations. The method of recording the sound signals on the tape determines the tracking and speed, and the equipment used for playback must be compatible with the variable characteristics with which the sound is recorded.   ·

There are a number of tracking characteristics determined by the recording equipment which are common to certain types of integral containers of the tape. Reel-to-reel tape can be recorded in a full-track mode, that is one sound track recorded across the full width of the tape; or two sound tracks each recorded on ½ of the width of the tape; or four sound tracks, each recorded on ¼ of the width of the tape. These are described as single, full, or one-track; two-track; or four-track. Terminology used to describe track configuration has changed from *AACR 1*. In *AACR 2*, half-track is the same as 2 track; quarter-track is the same as 4 track. The fractions refer to the portion of the whole used for each of the tracks.

A monophonic recording indicates that the sound is recorded from one main source. Mono recordings can be full- or 1-track or can be 2-track where half of the tape is used for one sound track recorded in one direction, and the other half of the tape is used for another sound track recorded in the other direction. A two-track mono reel-to-reel tape is played through on one track and the reel is turned over to play back the other sound track on the other half of the tape.

A stereophonic tape recording indicates that sound is recorded from two main sources. Stereo recordings cannot be full-track but may be two-track, four-track or, in the case of cartridge recordings, eight-tracks. Any given width of an eight-track stereo tape contains four different pieces of recorded information, with each of the four recorded from two main sources.

If determinable from information on the item or from playing the item, the track configuration, that is the number of tracks, and information about the mode of recording, either mono or stereo, should be given in the physical description. Rule 6.5C6. instructs the cataloger to give the number of tracks for tape recordings, unless the number of tracks is standard for the item. No standard number is suggested by the rules for reel-to-reel tape. The number of tracks by inference should then always be recorded, if known. A note to this rule defines the standard for cartridges as eight tracks and for cassettes as four tracks. If the number of tracks for these types of recordings differ from this standard, the number should be given.

Tape recording configurations and stereo and monographic tape formats are described in Fig. 4-1 and Fig. 4-2 below.

Fig. 4-1
Tape Recording Configurations*

Full Track

Half Track

Quarter Track

---

*From Wyman, Raymond, *Mediaware: Selection, Operation and Maintenance*, 2nd Ed. (c) 1969, 1976 Wm. C. Brown Company Publishers, Dubuque, Iowa. Reprinted by permission.

Fig. 4-2
Stereo and Monophonic Tape Formats*

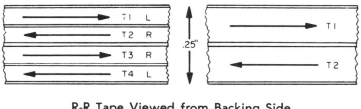

R-R Tape Viewed from Backing Side

Cassette Tape Viewed from Oxide Side

The width of sound tape also varies for the different types of integral containers. Reel-to-reel tape can be ¼-inch which is the most common or ½-inch. Cassette tapes are usually ⅛-inch-wide, and cartridges are usually ¼-inch-wide.

The speed at which sound is recorded also differs. Reel-to-reel tape is commonly recorded at 1⅞-, 3¾-, or 7½-inches per second. Generally speaking, the faster the speed and the wider the area for recording, the better the fidelity of the recording. Sound cassettes are generally recorded at 1⅞-inches per second, and cartridges are usually recorded at 3¾-inches per second.

Thickness of the tape also varies, but because this does not effect the equipment for playback, this is not described. The thickness of the tape determines the amount of tape that can be put on a reel or in a container. The length of the tape plus the speed determine the duration.

The physical characteristics of disc recordings are fairly standardized and do not present much problem for description. The basic types and characteristics are outlined in Fig. 4-3 (see page 78).

In addition to those physical characteristics of records summarized above, the characteristics of the "stereo" disc include 33⅓ rpm, 10-12 inches in diameter, and a playing time of approximately 50 minutes. The groove size on stereo recordings is .0007. Although stereo recordings can be played on a record player which is equipped with a stylus or needle appropriate for microgroove recordings, the difference in the size of the needle can cause wear on the recording and will not produce maximum sound fidelity. Ideally, stereo recordings should only be used with stereo equipment, although most libraries which circulate recordings have little control over their use. Discs are described in terms of duration, playing speed in rpms, groove characteristics which are not standard for the type of disc, including stereo for 33⅓ rpm discs, and other recording characteristics, if important for playback purposes. The final element to consider is the dimension of the disc.

---

*From Wyman, Raymond, *Mediaware: Selection, Operation and Maintenance*, 2nd Ed. (c) 1969, 1976 Wm. C. Brown Company Publishers, Dubuque, Iowa. Reprinted by permission.

Fig. 4-3
Physical Characteristics of Records*

	Standard	Transcription	Long Play	"45"	"16"
Speed in RPM	78	33	33	45	16
Grooves per Inch	110	110	250	250	400
Maximum Diameter	12 in/30 cm	16 in/41 cm	12 in/30 cm	7 in/17 cm	7 in/17 cm
Maximum Playing Time per Side	5 min	15 min	25 min	8 min	30 min
Needle Tip Radius	0.003 in 0.076 mm (standard)	0.003 in 0.076 mm (standard)	0.001 in 0.025 mm (microgroove)	0.001 in 0.025 mm (microgroove)	0.001 in 0.025 mm (microgroove)
Center Hole Diameter	¼ in/7 mm	¼ in/7 mm	¼ in/7 mm	1½ in/38 mm	1½ in/38 mm

There are two types of sound track film, one of which is archival and no longer made. This type is motion picture film on which sound has been recorded in grooves rather than magnetically or optically. Information about this type of recording can be given in a combination of information in the physical description and in the notes. However, few libraries collect this material. A more common type of sound track film is film on which only sound and no picture is recorded. As with other types of motion pictures, there are two methods of recording sound which determine the type of equipment needed for playback. Most sound tracks are recorded with optical sound. This information cannot be assumed, however, and should be given in the physical description according to 6.5C2. Examples of this description are as follows:

Physical description area

Sound recording on tape

1 sound cassette (18 min.) : 1 7/8 ips.

1 sound cassette (34 min.) : 3 3/4 ips.

3 sound cassettes (62 min.) : 1 7/8 ips, stereo.

1 sound cartridge (ca. 50 min.) : 3 3/4 ips, stereo.

1 sound tape reel (28 min.) : 3 3/4 ips, 2 track, mono. ; 5 in.

1 sound tape reel (25 min.) : 7 1/2 ips, 4 track, stereo. ; 7 in.

1 sound cassette (48 min.) : 1 7/8 ips + 1 teacher's guide.

---

*From Wyman, Raymond, *Mediaware: Selection, Operation and Maintenance*, 2nd Ed. (c) 1969, 1976 Wm. C. Brown Company Publishers, Dubuque, Iowa. Reprinted by permission.

Sound recording on disc

1 sound disc (42 min.) : 33 1/3 rpm, stereo. ; 12 in.

on side 1 of 1 sound disc (22 min.) : 33 1/3 rpm ; 12 in.

1 sound disc (48 min.) : 33 1/3 rpm, mono. ; 10 in.

1 sound disc (ca. 15 min.) : 45 rpm ; 7 in.

10 sound discs (449 min.) : 33 1/3 rpm, stereo. ; 12 in.

6.6. SERIES AREA

6.6B. SERIES STATEMENTS

Some sound recordings are published in series and fall into the categories described as series in the *AACR 2* Glossary. These are sometimes numbered and are recorded as instructed in 1.6. Other series, which are usually not numbered and are often not related in terms of content of individual items in the series, but are marketing devices of a publisher for a group of unrelated recordings, are recorded in the series area for this type of material. When a trade name is associated with a group of recordings and is not a functioning subdivision of a publisher, it is recorded as a series.

Series statements

. — (Modern American poetry criticism)

. — (Retrospect series)

. — (Recorded anthology of American music)

. — (Music from Ravinia ; v. 3)

If individual items in a set are cataloged separately, the title of the set can also be given as a series statement. If the set is part of another series, that can be the first series statement with the set title as a subseries statement.

6.7. NOTE AREA

Because of the importance of the publisher's number in identification of the item, LC has decided to put 6.7B19., notes on publishers' numbers, as the first note. This rule differs from other rules for recording numbers in that the note is to be prefaced by the name on the label.

Publisher's number note

World Records: SH116.

Blue Note: LT 987.

Nimbus: 2116.

Seraphim: S 60343.

Deutsche Grammophon: 2531199.

Folkways: 8772E.

London: 99451.

Historic Masters: HMB 8.

6.7B1. Nature or artistic form and medium of performance

Some of this information may be given in the title area and need not be repeated here. If omitted from the title area, usually because the information does not appear in the chief source(s) for the type of format, the information should be given here.

Form or medium note

Radio drama recorded from broadcast made Dec. 20, 1937.

Lecture with question and answer segments.

Vocal ensembles, songs, and harpsichord music.

For 2 trumpets, tympani, 2 violins, chorus and continuo.

Orchestral arrangements of arias from operas.

6.7B2. Language

If the language of the content differs from the language of the title in the description, it should be given in a note. Language(s) found in the accompanying material may also be important, but should be noted in relation to other notes for that material.

Language note

Sung in Latin.

Read in French with English translation following each poem.

Sung in English.

Each selection sung in original language.

6.7B3. Source of title proper

For a supplied title or for a title taken from a unifying element such as a container, information about the source should be given.

Source of title note

Title from container.

Title from accompanying material.

Title from distributor's catalog.

6.7B6. Statements of responsibility

Particularly because of the limitations placed upon the recording of performers' names in the body of the description, providing complete information about performers here is important. Unfortunately, there are no formal categories suggested. It is best to group these notes together with the names associated with similar functions in separate paragraphs and designate the relationship of each person or group named to the item being described. Other information related to those named in the statement of responsibility can also be given here and should be separated from notes related to performers. If contents notes can be related to performers, the information can be given there rather than in this note area.

Responsibility notes

Joan Sutherland, soprano ; New Philharmonia Orchestra, Richard Bonynge, conductor.

Lee Morgan, trumpet ; David "Fathead" Newman, tenor saxophone ; Cedar Walton, piano ; Ron Carter, bass ; Billy Higgins, drums.

Jessye Norman, Mirella Freni, Yvonne Minton, sopranos ; Ingvar Wixell, baritone ; Wladimiro Ganzarollik, bass ; BBC Symphony Orchestra and Chorus, Colin Davis, conductor.

Philadelphia String Quartet.

Aeolian String Quartet ; with Thea King, clarinet in first work.

Ed Ames with orchestra.

Lecture by the author.

Cadenza by Joachim.

Stuart Finley, narrator.

Arranged by Bruno Reibold.

Text of 4th movement by J. C. F. von Schiller.

6.7B7.   Edition and history
These notes should relate to the sound recording and not to the material in another format on which the recording is based. That information belongs in the previous note area, 6.7B6.

Edition and history note

Works realized at the Columbia-Princeton Electronic Music Center.

Recorded on the E. G. & G. Hook Organ, Church of Immaculate Conception, Boston.

Edited from the Pacem in Terris IV Convocation, Washington, D. C., Dec., 1975.

Recording of radio broadcast May 23, 1979.

"Direct disc recording, limited edition, recorded July 18 & 20, 1977 at M.G.M. Studio, Culver City, Calif."

6.7B9.   Publication, distribution, etc.
These notes should relate to the item in hand and not be confused with the history of previous recordings related to the one in hand.

Publication, etc. note

Issued by the British Institute of Recorded Sound in collaboration with EMI Records (The Gramophone Co.)

Previously issued as: Grammophon 022334.

Licensed from Erato: 70912.

6.7B10. Physical description
Notes given here should relate to the physical characteristics only of the disc, tape, etc., an integral container such as a cassette, or the container of the sound recording.

Physical description note

"Dolby processed"

Segments recorded at 3 3/4 ips for special effects.

Sound recorded on track 1 only.

Disc made of flexible plastic.

Although better included with the contents note, duration of individual parts can be given here.

Duration: Each selection ca. 5 min.

Durations on label.

Durations: 13 min. ; 6 min. ; 3 min., 52 sec.

6.7B11. Accompanying material
The location and type of textual accompanying material or other type of material and its characteristics can be described in detail in this note area.

Accompanying material note

Synopsis by E. Spielberg on container.

Booklet (128 p.; 14 cm.)

Program notes by Lionel Stater on container.

Program notes by Joan Chissell in English, German and French on container.

Booklet contains text in German and English.

Text of last work in German with English translations on container.

6.7B14. Audience
As with other chapters, the audience level or other audience characteristics can be given here if stated on any part of the item. The terms are best taken from the item itself.

Audience note

Intended audience: Continuing education for the legal profession.

Intended audience: Elementary grades.

For broadcast use only.

Made for use of American Armed Forces.

6.7B16. Other formats available

The use of this note should, in most libraries, be restricted to information about other formats of the same title which are available in the library. A separate entry for each format of each title is preferable, however, because if the information is given only in this type of note, it is difficult for the user to locate and interpret and does not provide for complete physical description of the format mentioned. Alluding to other formats in which an item is published is of interest to few users and can be found in reference sources.

Availability note

Also available as 1 sound tape reel (28 min.) : 3 3/4 ips, 2 track, mono. ; 5 in.

Also available as 1 sound disc (44 min.) : 33 1/3 rpm, stereo. ; 12 in.

6.7B17. Summary

Although this rule implies that summaries are less necessary for sound recordings than for other formats, they can provide valuable information and can be given for any material, musical or spoken word, for which there is a need. When the title and titles in contents notes do not sufficiently explain the type of material, the scope, the point of view of the material, and significant artistic characteristics, this information can be included in a summary. Also, a summary is often the most appropriate place to explain the relationship of those named in the statement of responsibility and notes which relate to responsibility, or those individuals and groups omitted from those two areas.

Summary note

Summary: Tom Bradley, Mayor of Los Angeles, calls for an urban recovery program. Points out federal government's neglect and offers remedies.

Summary: T. M. Aluko discusses themes in his novels focusing on the interaction between African culture and "imported" European culture.

Summary: Greek language instruction for the English speaking with phrases and sentences in each language.

6.7B18. Contents

A contents note with information as complete as possible, including statements of responsibility and duration, if available, is essential for sound recordings with collective titles which are cataloged as a unit. Titles used are titles proper taken from the chief source for the item.

Contents notes

Contents: Jerusalem blues — Careless love — Dippemouth blues — Ain't gonna give nobody none of my jelly roll — Dallas blues — Tin roof blues.

Contents: Tannhauser overture / Wagner — Der Freischutz overture / Weber — Merry Wives of Windsor overture / Nicolai Ruy — Blas overture, op. 95 / Mendelssohn — Hansel and Gretel overture / Humperdinck.

Contents: Les folles d'Espagne / M. Marais — Eight pieces / P. Hindemith — Fantasia in D. major / F. Kahlau — Sonata in A minor / C. P. E. Bach — Variations on a Swedish folktune / I. Dahl.

6.7B19. Notes on publishers' numbers

As previously mentioned, this note will be given as the first note by the Library of Congress and can also be placed first by other cataloging agencies.

6.7B21. "With" notes

When multipart items without a collective title are cataloged separately, as is the cataloger's option in 6.1G1., this note is essential. Although the example in *AACR 2* gives only the title proper, the cataloger can add the uniform title if important to the user.

With note

With: Suite for woodwinds and brasses, op. 4 in B flat major / Richard Strauss — Serenade for woodwinds, 2 horns and double bass, op. 57 / Richard Arnell.

With: Speech at the National Press Club luncheon, Washington, June 9, 1954 / C. S. Cameron.

6.9. SUPPLEMENTARY ITEMS

These are to be described according to 1.9. which outlines the three ways to handle accompanying material. Most supplementary items found with sound recordings can be adequately described as accompanying material in the physical description, with additional details put in the notes related to accompanying material under 6.7B11. Minor items not mentioned in the physical description or even in complete descriptions can also be included in notes under 6.7B11. Multilevel description is not recommended.

6.10. ITEMS MADE UP OF SEVERAL TYPES OF MATERIAL

Even with sound recordings accompanied by several different types of material, perhaps a book, a script, and extensive commentary, they should be described as sound recordings when the main burden of intellectual and artistic content is assigned to the recording.

6.11. NONPROCESSED SOUND RECORDINGS

These directions for sound recordings which are locally produced, not formally published and not available for distribution, are similar to the rules for graphics and other materials which exist in unique, single copies only. Since they often lack titles, one must be supplied. Because they are not formally published, no information can be given in the publication area. Any available information can be included in the notes area, in the order and manner suggested for commercial sound recordings.

EXAMPLES:
Descriptive Cataloging of Sound Recordings

Tchaikovsky, Peter Illich, 1840-1893.
    [The nutcracker. Suite]
    Nutcracker suite, op. 71a [sound recording] / Tchaikovsky. —
[New York] : Columbia, [1961]

    On side 2 of 1 sound disc (21 min.) : 33 1/3 rpm, stereo. ;
12 in.

    Columbia: MS 6193.
    New York Philharmonic, Leonard Bernstein, conductor.
    Program notes on liner.
    Contents: Miniature overture (3 min., 16 sec.) — Danses
characteristics (11 min.) — Waltz of the flowers (6 min.)
    With: Peter and the wolf / Prokofiev.

    I. New York Philharmonic. II. Bernstein, Leonard, 1918-
III. Title.

Musical recording, lacking a collective title, with parts described separately. Uniform title, title proper, and physical description refer to the part only. Publisher's number as first note according to LC practice. Contents note with durations as stated on item. GMD omitted after uniform title, according to LC practice.

———————

Stallman, Lou.
    Let's act as consumers [sound recording] / original words and
music by Lou Stallman and Bob Susser. — Roslyn Heights,
N.Y. : Stallman-Susser Educational Systems, 1972.

    1 sound disc (ca. 45 min.) : 33 1/3 rpm ; 12 in.

    Stallman-Susser Educational Systems: LPED 129A.
    Songs sung by Lou Stallman.
    Produced by Lou Stallman and Bob Susser.
    Teacher's guide on container.
    Intended audience: Children.
    Summary: A one-act play that deals with purchasing to teach
consumer awareness.
    Contents: The book sale — I'm a consumer — More for my
money — Here are some rules — I want what I want — Consumer
test.

    I. Susser, Bob. II. Title.

Spoken word recording not needing a uniform title. Statement of responsibility from the item. Responsibility notes related to performer and production. Description of accompanying material in a note rather than in physical description. Audience mentioned on program notes. Contents note from label.

    DeRegniers, Beatrice Schenk.
      May I bring a friend? [sound recording] / [book by Schenk de Regniers and Montresor ; composed and sung by Albert Hangue]. — Weston, Conn. : Weston Woods, 1973.

    1 sound cassette (7 min.) : 1 7/8 ips, 2 track, mono.

    Weston Woods: LTR 164C.
    Text from the book of the same title published by Atheneum, 1964.
    Side 1 with inaudible signal, side 2 with audible signal.
    Summary: The king and queen are surprised at the strange friends a little boy brings to visit each day of the week.

    I. Montresor, Beni. II. Hague, Albert. III. Title.

Entry is under author prominently named on container. Complete form of the name found on the material. Composer named in statement of responsibility because of importance of contribution to content of sound recording. Use partly determined by use of automatic advance signals indicated in note about physical description. Summary useful for children's materials.

    Hale, Lucretia P.
      The Peterkin papers [sound recording] / by Lucretia P. Hale. — New York : Caedmon Records, 1973.

    1 sound disc (52 min.) : 33 1/3 rpm, stereo. ; 12 in.

    Caedmon: TC 1377.
    Read by Cathleen Nesbitt.
    Intended audience: Elementary grades.
    Contents: The lady who put salt in her coffee (12 min.) — About Elizabeth Eliza's piano (2 min., 37 sec.) — The Peterkins try to become wise (7 min.) — The Peterkins at home (3 min., 49 sec.) — The Peterkins snowed-up (11 min.) — The Peterkins' picnic (15 min.)

    I. Nesbitt, Cathleen. II. Title.

Entry under prominently named author of content. Performer named in note and given added entry. Audience on item. Duration of entire recording given in physical description, duration of individual items also included in contents note.

Wagner, Linda.
    William Carlos Williams [sound recording] / lecturer, Linda
Wagner. — Deland, Fla. : E. Edwards, 1972.

    1 sound cassette (28 min.) : 1 7/8 ips, 2 track, mono. — (Modern
American poetry criticism)

    Everett Edwards: 808.

        I. Title. II. Series.

Entry under lecturer. Series named and traced. No summary needed because
content clear from the body of the description.

    The World of marches [sound recording]. — North Hollywood,
    Calif. : Bomar Records, [19--]

    1 sound disc (ca. 50 min.) : 33 1/3 rpm ; 12 in.

    Bomar: 2051.
    City of Los Angeles Concert Band, Gabriel Bartold, conductor.
    Contents: National emblem / Bagley — Aguero / Franco — March
from Aida / Verdi-Bartold — British Eighth / Elliott — French
national defile / Turlet — Einzugs march / Strauss — Entry of the
gladiators / Fucik-Laurendeau — Parade of the charioteers /
Ronza — Colonel Bogey / Alford — Third of February march /
Roncal — Under the double eagle / Wagner.

Musical recording with a collective title. Names of parts in the contents notes with
composers as they appear on the item. Added entries could be given for
individual pieces if important to users.

V
Description of Motion Pictures and Videorecordings

AACR 2 CHAPTER 7: MOTION PICTURES AND VIDEORECORDINGS

7.0. GENERAL RULES

7.0A. SCOPE

The scope of this chapter includes many different types of images on film which simulate motion and electronic images on videotape which record motion. Films of varying length, from short film clips, to full-length theatrical productions, to films in series, are included. Sound track films are not included because they do not contain images, but only record sound. These are films with only a magnetic or optical sound track. Single-concept film loops, standard 8mm, and super 8mm films in cartridges and on reels are included.

Many libraries have established their own procedures for accessing films. School libraries and public libraries often omit film and videorecordings from the local collection. Films are cataloged, stored, and circulated from a central agency, either a school district film center, district media center, central public library, branch, or state library film collection. Many universities also have central film services. Most of these agencies do not provide complete descriptive cataloging for their materials. A typical film catalog will enter the film under title, give a brief synopsis, and index the collection by a limited number of subject categories. Many of these agencies, particularly those which rent films and publish catalogs of their rental holdings, may want to continue their current practices.

Providing bibliographic access in a unified media catalog, using the standard descriptive techniques, however, can only increase their availability through more detailed description. Many of the notes and added entries, based on the description, given for motion pictures and videorecordings provide valuable information for the user. They enable the user to identify these materials from many points of interest by providing information which is often lacking in the typical film catalog in book form. If the cataloging done by film agencies was adequate from the point of view of different types of users, these rules would not be necessary. In most cases, however, these rules provide more information than most of the presently used, locally developed methods. If a film service wants to continue publishing a catalog in book form, the entry in the book catalog can be taken from the descriptive cataloging done according to *AACR 2*. In developing the book catalog entry, the cataloger can simply eliminate any information from the *AACR 2* entry which is not deemed necessary. A synopsis or summary of the film content is provided for in AACR 2, and this can be used as the book catalog entry. Also, because the records done according to *AACR 2* are machine-readable, the records can be entered into a computerized system, and the film library can produce a film catalog using computer techniques.

7.0B. SOURCES OF INFORMATION

7.0B1. Chief source of information

The chief source which is the preferred source for most descriptive areas is the item itself and the container, if it is an integral part, that is, if the film or videorecording cannot be physically separated from the container for playback purposes. This would include a cassette or cartridge housing a film or videorecording. Bibliographic information can appear at any point in the production, and catalogers should be alert to the fact that to catalog this type of format adequately, it is necessary to scan the complete item to be sure that information which may appear at the end of the film or videorecording can be considered. Title frames, credits, and other valuable information appear at the beginning and at the end of the material. If called-for information does not appear in the chief source, it can be supplied from other sources listed:

- accompanying material in text form including scripts, press books, publicity, study guides
- the container including blurbs permanently affixed to the film can, the case which holds the videotape, and the cover of the videodisc
- other sources including publisher's catalogs, press releases, selection tools, etc.

7.0B2. Prescribed sources of information

For each area of description, there are given prescribed source(s) from which the information can be taken without bracketing the information. Examine the chief source first, and extract from the chief source(s) information for the following areas:

Area 1   Title and statement of responsibility
     2   Edition
     3   Publication, distribution
     6   Series

For information not found in the chief source, examine accompanying material(s) for information for the following areas:

Area 2   Edition
     4   Publication, distribution, etc.
     6   Series

If not found in any of the above, take information from any source for the remaining areas:

Area 5   Physical description
     7   Notes
     8   Standard number and terms of availability

Any information required by the chosen level of description can be taken from any source if the information is bracketed. Prefer the prescribed sources in the order given, in case of conflicting information for any of the descriptive elements.

7.1. TITLE AND STATEMENT OF RESPONSIBILITY AREA

Record the title proper as instructed in 1.1B. The prescribed source(s) of information are the chief source(s), including the item itself, or lacking information there, accompanying text and material, the container, or other sources. Information taken from other than the item itself must be bracketed. Rules in 1.1B1. cover problems associated with the presentation of film and video titles. For alternative titles, see 1.1B1. For items in which the title appears in two or more languages, see 1.1B8. and 1.1D. for parallel titles. For a film made originally in a language other than English and dubbed in English, the cataloger should record the English title if given in the chief source in that language. The language of the original, if given on the film, should be given following the GMD, as a parallel title. If only given in another language, use the other language title as the title proper, do not translate it. If the sound track is recorded in another language and the title appears in that language in the chief source, which it usually does, the original language of the title would appear in the title proper. The English title, if it does appear, can be recorded as a parallel title. If the film has English subtitles, that fact can be given in a note. Other title information following the GMD is covered in 1.1E.

Title proper

Ah — we humans [motion picture]

Arthur Penn films Little big man [motion picture]

Austria and the Lipizzaner horses [motion picture]

George Segal [motion picture]

Parallel title

Visit to the sepulcher [motion picture] = Visitatio sepulchri. —

Afterlife [videorecording] = Apres la vie. —

Other title information

America in 1968 [motion picture] : people and culture. —

Asbestos [motion picture] : the way to dusty death. —

Glory was, glory is! [motion picture] : the Peloponnesus of Greece. —

Spirit catcher [videorecording] : the art of Betye Saar. —

7.1C. OPTIONAL ADDITION. GENERAL MATERIAL DESIGNATION

Add the GMD [motion picture] or [videorecording] following the title, before parallel titles in other languages, and before other title information or subtitles.

7.1F.   STATEMENTS OF RESPONSIBILITY

Record in the statement of responsibility individuals or groups named in the chief source of information if they are "of major importance to the film and the interests of the cataloguing agency." "Give all other statements of responsibility in the notes." The chief source is the film or videorecording itself, including beginning and ending portions. If persons responsible are not named there, but are named in other sources acceptable as substitutes for the chief source, see 7.0B1.; they can be named here if deemed necessary for the item and for the library. Any statement of responsibility appearing prominently in the item should be included here as instructed in 1.1F1. Statements appearing in other sources can be included if bracketed. Statements not chosen for inclusion in this area can and probably should be given in a note. The amount of information given in this area depends upon the judgment of the cataloger and policy set by the library.

7.1F2.

If the nature of the relationship of groups or individuals is given on the item or in other acceptable sources, that phrase or word indicating the relationship should be recorded in this area. If the relationship is not given in the source from which the information is taken but is found elsewhere, a word or phrase can be added in brackets for clarification. Give both the production agency and the organization for which an item is produced if they are both named.

Notes related to the statements of responsibility are discussed in 7.7B6. Individuals and groups who are related to the production in either capacity and are omitted from the statement of responsibility can be named in notes. The cast is not named in a statement of responsibility, but in a note headed "Cast:." Those who are associated with the artistic and technical production, not named in the statement of responsibility area, can be included in the notes, preceded by the word "Credits:." Organizations or individuals related to the production who could be candidates for inclusion in the statement of responsibility, but are omitted from that area, can be named in notes related to the statement of responsibility. See examples under 7.7B6. for notes relating to this area.

The Library of Congress will give all major credits for individuals and groups found in the chief source of information. Here they will name producers, directors, writers, and others responsible for the technical or artistic aspect of a film, such as an animator or photographer for a travelog. Other libraries may wish to put some of this information in notes.

Full statement of responsibility

Instructing the disabled worker on the job [videorecording] / United States Office of Education with the cooperation of the United States Office of Vocational Rehabilitation ; made by Caravel Films. —

Manufacturing [videorecording] : IBM / Academic counselors of the College of Arts and Sciences with the cooperation of the Arts and Sciences Placement Office, Indiana University ; made by Indiana University Radio and Television Service. —

(Example continues on page 92)

Manufacturing [videorecording] : IBM / made by Indiana University Radio and Television Service. —

Alternative statement of responsibility for above example.

Prepared with academic counselors of the college of Arts and Sciences with the cooperation of the Arts and Sciences Placement Office, Indiana University.

Note related to statement.

Statement of responsibility

Young children with special needs [videorecording] : motor skills / Virginia Commonwealth University in cooperation with the Virginia Association for Retarded Citizens, Developmental Disabilities Advisory Council, and Central Virginia Television Corporation. —

A Teacher in reflection [videorecording] / National Institute of Mental Health ; made by UCLA Media Center. —

Step by step [motion picture] / District no. 9 New York City Board of Education ; made by Steve Campus Productions, Inc. —

Seidelman, Susan.
Yours truly, Andrea G. Stern [motion picture] / by Susan Seidelman. —

Creedman, Nancy.
Indian crafts [motion picture] : Hopi, Navajo, and Iroquois / by Nancy Creedman. —

Creative storytelling techniques [videorecording] : mixing the media / with Dr. Caroline Feller Bauer. —

The Boy from Kalihi [motion picture] / Ariyoshi for Governor, a committee ; made by Media Group. —

7.1G. ITEMS WITHOUT A COLLECTIVE TITLE

If more than one item is recorded on videotape or other motion picture format, it is best to describe each item separately and link the descriptions with a note as instructed in 7.1G4. However, if they are conceptually related, or related in terms of the person or group responsible for the intellectual content, or if they have a collective title, they can be described as a unit.

7.2. EDITION AREA

7.2B3. Optional Addition.

The cataloger can optionally add a statement in this area, enclosed in brackets, concerning the edition or changes from a previous version of a film or videorecording. LC has opted not to apply this rule. If information is given on the item, or otherwise known, about the version of the item in hand, it can be given in a note under 7.7B7. which relates to the edition and history of the item. Because these relationships are difficult to describe succinctly, putting the information in a note enables the cataloger to more adequately record the information. See examples under 7.7B7.

7.4. PUBLICATION, DISTRIBUTION, ETC., AREA

Without bracketing, information in this area can be taken from the chief source, the item itself, or from accompanying material. All of the places and all of the names, usually of groups, associated with the publication, distribution, and release of the item should be included here. Also, those production agencies and producers not named in the statement of responsibility can be named here. The latter would be particularly appropriate here if the production agency or producer were not mentioned prominently in the item or if the library had decided not to include this type of information in the statement of responsibility for cataloging any of the items from this chapter.

Items made originally as films and issued on video formats should be described as videorecordings. Details related to the statement of responsibility and publication may relate to their origination, and details concerning their manufacture and distribution will probably relate to their recording on videotape or videodisc. Many productions are now being offered in both types of formats. The format in hand is the one which concerns the cataloger.

Rules for punctuation for this area, which often contains several places, several names, and several dates, can be found in the rules for punctuation in 7.4A1. and in the rules for punctuation for this area in 1.4A1., the general rules. Examples for this area in both Chapter 7 and Chapter 1 will be helpful.

7.4C. PLACE OF PUBLICATION, DISTRIBUTION, ETC.

If determinable, the place of each of the agencies named should be recorded in this area. In addition, there is an option in rule 1.4C7. to add the address of any one or several of these if it is deemed necessary by the library. For small organizations which are difficult to locate in reference sources, this option may provide this information.

7.4D. NAME OF PUBLISHER, DISTRIBUTOR, ETC.

Because there are often several names associated with motion pictures and videorecordings in these capacities, an indication of the function of each of the names is necessary. This can be done using a phrase from the item as instructed in 1.4D3. or by optionally adding a statement of the function according to 1.4E. and 1.4E1.

Rule 1.4E1. gives the cataloger four choices for a statement of function of those named in this area. The producer is defined in the *AACR 2* Glossary as "the person with final responsibility for the making of a motion picture, including business aspects, management of the production, and the commercial success of the film." This is a much broader definition of function than the one usually associated with a film producer who would be named in the credits. Usually, a producer will be named in this area only when a production company is not named. The producer, if named here, would be responsible for all of the functions of a company. Some short films, but relatively few major productions, result from this type of activity.

If a library has chosen to record the name of one or more of the persons or groups associated with publication, distribution, etc. in the statement of responsibility, the name(s) must be repeated in this area. It can be given in shortened form, if it appears in full in the statement of responsibility. The need to record these names here also makes it less imperative to record the name in the statement of responsibility area. It is assumed by most film users that groups responsible for publication and production often have some responsibility for content.

7.4F. DATE OF PUBLICATION, DISTRIBUTION, ETC.

Date(s) of publication, etc. of the item in hand should be recorded. Rule 1.4F4. instructs the cataloger to give dates associated with the different functions of the various agencies named, after the place and name to which they apply.

The date of the original production of a film or video presentation may be important to the user. Rule 7.4F2. instructs the cataloger to provide this information in a note according to rule 7.7B9. Videorecordings which were originally offered in film, prior to the publication in the video format, will become more common. Information about the original offering can be recorded in a note.

7.4G. PLACE OF MANUFACTURE, NAME OF MANUFACTURER, DATE OF MANUFACTURER

If the publisher is unknown, this information should be given. It is usually not necessary for films, but it may be the only information available for some videorecordings.

Publication, distribution, etc., area

Asbestos [motion picture] : the way to dusty death / ABC News, Documentary Unit. — New York : ABC Learning Resources, 1978.

Apollo 15 [videorecording] : in the mountains of the moon / National Aeronautics and Space Administration ; made by A-V Corporation. — Washington : NASA : Distributed by National Audiovisual Center, 1979.

Read/think [motion picture] : the art of reading / Ralph Lopatin Productions. — Mt. Laurel, N.J. : Learning Inc., 1979.

Red alert [motion picture] / United States Federal Aviation Administration ; made by Communication Group Inc. — Washington : The Administration : Distributed by National Audiovisual Center, 1979.

Stage fright [motion picture] / Centron Corporation. — Lawrence, Kan. : Centron Films, 1979.

The Nguba connection [videorecording] / WGBH Educational Foundation. — Boston : WGBH Educational Foundation, Distribution Office, 1978.

Personalizing reading for children [videorecording] / California State Department of Education ; made by KTEH/TV/Veriation Films. — Bloomington, Ind. : Agency for Instructional Television [distributor], 1977.

7.5. PHYSICAL DESCRIPTION AREA

The physical characteristics of two major types of nonprint materials collected by libraries need to be considered in constructing a complete and accurate physical description. Films and videotape or videodisc both record moving visuals and usually record sound, but their characteristics are different.

Film

Film is described in terms of its base, the container of the base, the duration, unusual projection requirements, sound characteristics, color, unusual projection speed, and width. The same type of base, cellulose acetate, with a top coat, emulsion, and backing, is found in all types of motion picture film, so that the term *film* is adequate for its description. Early films were made of cellulose nitrate which is highly flammable and no longer used. Film of varying widths is housed on or in several types of containers, open reels, cartridges, and cassettes. In projection, open reel film passes through a projector, is taken up on another open reel and must be rewound. Film in a closed cartridge is usually housed on a closed loop mechanism, that is, one end of the film is connected to the other and the film plays continuously. It does not go through a rewind process. Films housed in cassettes actually travel from one reel to another within the cassette. As with audiotape, these must be rewound, but do so automatically within the cassette. They do not play continuously.

These are generic applications of the terms. There are some companies, like Kodak, however, which package films in an enclosed reel-to-reel container which they refer to as a cartridge. These require a specific type of equipment for playback, and in this case, the name of the type of cartridge, e.g., Kodak Supermatic, which is actually a cassette, will have to be specified in the physical description or in a note. Generally, the term *cartridge* implies a continuous loop. Continuous loop cartridges, usually housing film which is 8mm-wide, come with film of varying length and in cartridges of different sizes to accommodate the length of the film. Projection equipment differs in its capacity to accommodate cartridges of different sizes, containing varying lengths of 8mm film. It is necessary to indicate these characteristics in the description of the film, either in a note, in the physical description area, or in a combination of information in both areas so that the user of the catalog record will know the projection requirements.

In addition, cartridges manufactured by some companies can only be played back on equipment which they manufacture. Technicolor, Inc. manufactures equipment to play back 8mm cartridges. Several other companies also manufacture equipment compatible with this type of cassette. Fairchild Camera and Instrument Corporation manufacturer cartridges and playback equipment to accommodate their cassettes of varying length. A Kodak projector must be used to play back the Kodak Supermatic cassette-cartridge. Characteristics of the software are the concern of the cataloger, but if only one type of equipment can be used for playback, the name of that equipment should be given in a note.

If characteristics of the film require special projection capabilities, this can be included in the physical description according to rule 7.5C2. Equipment can be specified in a note, according to rule 7.7B10. For film cartridges which are commonly accommodated by equipment produced by several manufacturers, but where this equipment can accommodate only certain sizes of cartridges (determined by the length of the film held by the cartridge), the length of the film can be recorded in a note according to 7.7B10b.

Sound is considered to be integral to motion pictures and is simply indicated as the presence or absence of sound in the physical description. Sound can be recorded on film optically or magnetically. Some projectors accommodate both types of sound tracks; others play back only one. Almost all 8mm film with sound contains a magnetic sound track; almost all 16mm film contains an optical sound track. If the item in hand differs from the standard, the information should be given in a note.

Sound and silent motion pictures are photographed at different speeds, 16 frames per second for silent and 24 frames per second for sound films. If sound is indicated, it is assumed that the film was photographed at the standard speed for sound; if the film is described as silent, it is assumed that it was photographed at the standard speed for silent films. If this is not the case, the different speed should be noted. A film made at the speed for silent films can be played back on a projector for sound films, but the images will pass through the projector more rapidly than intended and produce a speeded-up visual.

Film width also varies. The most common widths in multimedia collections are 8mm and 16mm. It is also produced in 35mm, 70mm, and 105mm. Generally, the larger the image on the film, the better the projected image. Film which is 8mm-wide comes in two forms, standard 8mm and super 8mm. The size of the image for super 8 is larger than it is for standard 8. Most 8mm film produced today uses the larger image and is, therefore, super 8mm.

Figure 5-1 represents the types of film most commonly found in libraries for which *AACR 2* would be used.

Videorecording

Videotapes are described in terms of the integral container of the videotape, including either cartridge, cassette, or reel; videodiscs are described in terms of the duration, sound characteristics, color, and playing speed. The tape width for videorecordings and the disc size for videodiscs are the final elements of the physical description. Like film, all videotapes contain a similar base, usually polyester with a topcoat, a magnetic oxide layer, and a backing. The specific designation for videotape, beginning with the prefix "video," is combined with one of the terms appropriate to describe the container of the tape, cassette, or reel. The videodisc has the magnetic properties associated with videotape, but is more similar to a disc sound recording in terms of the characteristics of its base. The technology related to the retrieval of the visual and sound recorded magnetically on tape and disc are dissimilar.

Fig. 5-1
Motion Picture Formats*

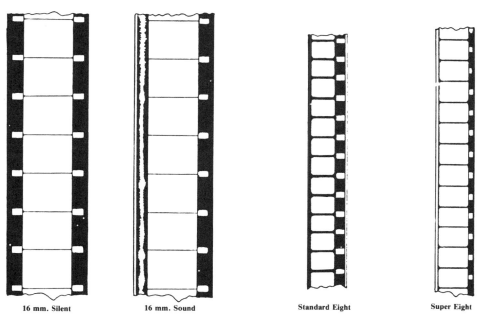

| 16 mm. Silent | 16 mm. Sound | Standard Eight | Super Eight |

*From Wyman, Raymond, *Mediaware: Selection, Operation, and Maintenance*, 2nd Ed. (c) 1969, 1976 Wm. C. Brown Company Publishers, Dubuque, Iowa. Reprinted by permission.

Open reel videotape was the first developed and collected by libraries. The tape is produced in different widths, ¼-inch, ½-inch, 1-inch, and 2-inch. As with film, the larger the image, the better the picture. Most broadcast tape and original professional production on videotape are done on 2-inch tape, which is recorded in a quadraplex mode. Quadraplex recordings require quadraplex playback equipment. Videotape on widths other than 2-inch tape uses the helical scan mode of recording. It is assumed that tape other than 2-inch is helical scans and that 2-inch tape is quadraplex. Libraries which collect master tapes, from which others are duplicated, collect 2-inch tape which can be reproduced in any of the other tape formats.

The first type of tape collected by libraries, other than those with large collections of master tapes, was the ½-inch, reel-to-reel tape. The Electronics Industry Association of Japan, which represents the manufacturers of video equipment, developed a standard, the EIAJ standard, which insured that most ½-inch videotape can be played back on most videorecorder-players. For ½-inch tape there are two standards, one for regular equipment and one for portable equipment. The only difference is in the size of the reel. The smaller reel, used for portable equipment, can be played back on regular size, standard equipment, however. Many libraries have collections of this type of tape and do some local production with studio or portable equipment which is added to their collections.

When ¾-inch tape, enclosed in videocassettes, was developed, many libraries began collecting pre-recorded tape in this format because of the ease of operation of this equipment. There is a standard (EIAJ) for this type of tape which is called the "U" standard. As with the ½-inch reel-to-reel, there is also a different size cassette for the portable equipment. The smaller cassettes for the portable recorders can be played back on both portable recorder-players and the standard size recorders and players.

For both ½-inch reel-to-reel and ¾-inch cassette recordings, playback is possible on equipment manufactured by many different Japanese and American companies. With 1-inch reel-to-reel and ½-inch cassettes, this is not the case. Equipment with competing technologies require different types of tape reels and cassettes. Type "C" tape is used with Sony, Ampex, and NEC 1. equipment. Type "C" tape, with "B" wind, and with the oxide side out is used for Bosch-Fernseh. Few libraries collect 1-inch tape.

The two major types of ½-inch cassette tape are the VHS format and the Beta format. Marketed for the home video market rather than the commercial market, these two types are being collected and circulated by libraries. Several manufacturers produce equipment to be used with each of these types, although Sony is usually associated with the Beta format and Panasonic with the VHS. The tape should be described in terms of its standard (VHS or Beta) rather than a specific trade name of the manufacturer of a particular piece of equipment. This is particularly true of VHS which can be used with Panasonic, RCA, Phillips, Magnavox, and equipment manufactured by several other companies.

During the first week of 1982, major Japanese manufacturers announced that they are developing a new standard for video-cassettes. This new standard cassette promises to be much smaller than the current U matic ¾-inch tape cassette and the ½-inch Beta and VHS cassettes. Marketing of the new miniature cassette and equipment for recording and playback has been announced for 1985. If the technical qualities of the product measure up to those of the products currently on the market, this format may capture a large portion of the home and library market.

There are currently two different recording and playback technologies in the videodisc field. One uses a diamond stylus to decode the magnetic signals imbedded on the disc, and the other uses a laser technology. The laser technology of DiscoVision was developed by MCA Phillips and is used with Magnavox Magnavision. RCA SelectaVision uses the stylus. Obviously, the software of these different types must be used with its own type of equipment. Other manufacturers are developing equipment which will probably be compatible with one or the other. No standards have yet been developed in this fast-changing field, and it is quite likely that other types of discs will be forthcoming. The best way to describe the discs which are currently available is with the term applied to the software by the producer.

The duration of a videorecording depends upon the length of the tape or the size of the disc and the speed at which it is recorded. Most reel-to-reel tape is recorded at a standard speed which does not have to be described. Most ¾-inch tape is also recorded at the same speed. However, the original equipment manufactured for use with the ½-inch cassettes of both the Beta and VHS formats uses a different speed from the newer "extended play" cassettes which run over one hour. Some equipment can accommodate both the regular speed and the extended play speed, but some cannot. These tape characteristics should be described.

There are other characteristics which should also be noted. The presence or absence of sound should be indicated for videorecordings. Video formats can contain more than one channel for sound and, therefore, may have more than one soundtrack. This too should be noted. The presence of color is not controlled by the type of tape stock used, but by the equipment with which the images are recorded on the tape. Presence of color should be noted. A color videorecording can be played back on equipment which is not color sensitive and will appear in black and white.

Physical description area

Motion pictures

1 film cartridge (28 min.) : sd., col. ; super 8 mm.

1 film loop (3 min., 22 sec.) : si., col. ; standard 8 mm.

1 film reel (22 min.) : sd., col. ; 16 mm.

1 film reel (34 min.) : sd., col. ; 35 mm.

3 film reels (110 min.) : sd., col. ; 70 mm.

1 film reel (15 min.) : sd., col. ; 16 mm. + 1 script + 1 study guide. − (Inner circle series)

1 film reel (11 min.) : sd., col. ; 16 mm. + 1 teacher's guide. − (Classic tales retold)

Physical description area

Videorecordings

1 videoreel (18 min.) : sd., b&w ; ½ in.

1 videoreel (22 min.) : sd., col. ; 2 in.

1 videoreel (Helical scan) (40 min.) ; sd., col. ; 2 in.

1 videocassette (30 min.) : sd., col. ; ¼ in.

1 videocassette (38 min.) : sd., col. ; ¾ in.

1 videocassette (25 min.) : sd., col. ; ½ in.

1 videocassette (Type C-B wind) (20 min.) : sd., col. ; ½ in.

1 videodisc (SelectaVision) (35 min.) : sd., col. ; 1500 rpm : 10 in.

1 videodisc (MCA DiscoVision) (22 min.) : sd., col. ; 1800 rpm : 12 in.

7.6. SERIES AREA

Motion pictures and videorecordings may appear in series which should be indicated at the end of the physical description. Most series are not numbered, but items within a series often carry an indication of placement within the series.

Often, items cataloged according to rules in this chapter are parts taken from other types of presentations, but are not actually a published series. This type of information can be indicated in the notes area related to the statement of responsibility, or related to the edition and history of the presentation.

Series statements

. — (Information processing and the computer ; unit 10) (The Computer as a tool ; module 2)

. — (Science rock) (Schoolhouse rock)

. — (Milton Freedman speaking ; lecture 8)

. — (Mechanical maintenance training ; module 14)

. — (The Six wives of Henry VIII ; 2)

. — (Horizon)

Although this chapter does not provide for separate notes related to the series, information not presented in the series can be given in notes related to edition and history under 7.7B7.

Note related to history and series

Program 7 in a television series for parents and professionals.

University of Michigan Media Library program, no. 60.

Part of ABC afterschool special series.

7.7. NOTE AREA

7.7B1. Nature of form
Many different types of notes are recommended and necessary for complete description of materials in these formats. The wide variety of content characteristics can be indicated according to 7.7B1. If a motion picture or videorecording is prepared for a different type of presentation such as a filmed opera or stage play, this should be indicated.

Form note

Film version of staged opera.

News broadcast.

Excerpts from film by producer.

Original TV play.

7.7B3,4,5. Title notes
Because of the various sources of title information and the use of several different titles for these productions, notes concerning the source of the title proper used in the description, variations in the titles given in different sources, and parallel titles in other languages can help to clarify and uniquely identify the item in hand.

Title notes

"Associated Press special report"
Original title: Search for the origin of our
species.

Title at end of film.

Title from container.

Original title: California's coast, the sunset shore.

7.7B6. Statements of responsibility

Libraries which choose to omit from the statement of responsibility individuals and groups named on the item but not considered to be named prominently, not named in chief source, or not deemed important for the library users should make liberal use of this type of notes.

Notes related to the statement of responsibility, including players, performers, narrators, cast, and lists of credits for those associated with the artistic and technical aspects of the production, can be invaluable information, particularly for those engaged in the study of the art of the medium. Using a formal note, prefaced by a term which groups those names, is an aid to the user in differentiating the functions of the people who should be named. Within each category, specific functions, particularly those mentioned prominently in the item, should be recorded.

Additional information about a person named in the credits can also be presented in the summary. A narrator, an interviewer, a person interviewed, or other relationship of an individual or group to the presentation can be explained in the summary.

Statement of responsibility notes

Sponsored by the National Petroleum Institute.

Made in cooperation with Coast Community College District and the University of California at San Diego.

Made by Film Images, Inc.

Made by A-V Corp.

In cooperation with School of Agriculture and Natural Resources, California Polytechnic State University, San Luis Obispo.

Made by Biomedical Media Production Unit.

Cast notes

Cast: Brad Dourif, Frank Converse, William Daniels, Stephen Elliott, Rue Clanahan.

Cast: Laurie Hendler, Kevin King Cooper, Annrae Walterhouse, Robbie Rist, Tim Reid, Beverly Archer.

Credit notes

Credits: Producer, Robert Chenault ; director, Arthur Lubin ; writer, Ann Elder.

Credits: Director, Otto Sacher.

Credits: Directors, Mick Jackson, David Kennard ; writer, James Burke.

Narrator: Mike Wallace.
Credits: Producer, Marion Coldin.

Credits: Director and adapter, Gene Deitch.

7.7B7. Edition and history

Information related to the history of the production which does not fit into other categories of notes can be given here. Information about material in another format, related to the production can also be given here.

Edition and history notes

Revised version of motion picture issued in 1964 under the same title.

Originally shown on TV series The World we live in.

Correlated with the book Behavior of exceptional children.

Originally shown on CBS program entitled 60 minutes.

Shorter version (14 min.) issued under title: A Faculty feeling.

Based on the book of the same title by Antoine de Saint Exupery.

Based on the book by the same title by Barbara K. Walker.

7.7B9. Publication, distribution, etc., and date

Information that relates to the publication facts of the item in hand can be given here. Information about publication, release, and distribution of an original or related version can also be helpful in these notes.

Publication, etc. notes

Issued in 1965 as a 16 mm. motion picture.

First released in 1976.

Released in France in 1977.

Also distributed in Canada by National Film Board of Canada.

7.7B10. Physical description

If information about the physical characteristics cannot be given succinctly or do not fit into the pattern indicated in the physical description area for the format, it can be given in the notes area. Any characteristic which is not typical of the format as it is described in the physical description, any characteristic which must be known in order to use the item but which is not related specifically enough in the physical description, or any other characteristic which would dictate the item's use should appear here.

Notes for motion pictures

Use with Kodak Supermatic projector.

Use with Fairchild film cartridge projector.

Silent film at the speed for sound, 24 fr. per sec.

Magnetic sound track.

Use with standard 8 mm. loop projector.

Notes for videorecordings

EIAJ standard.

Beta standard.

U standard.

VHS standard.

Type C-B wind cassette.

RCA SelectaVision.

Extended play tape.

Quadraplex recording.

Sound recorded on Channel 1 only, Channel 2 for student response.

7.7B11. Accompanying material

Accompanying material can be named and optionally described in the physical description area. Any amplification of information given in that area can be given in notes. These notes are particularly important for educational material.

Notes about accompanying material

With leader's guide, 20 worksheets, and book, The Silent messages (152 p.) by Albert Mehrabian.

With 2 instructor's guides, 50 student workbooks, and 12 transparencies.

With script and guide.

Study guide contains script.

With teacher's handbook, lesson plans, 25 activity sheets, and 25 music sheets.

7.7B16. Other formats available

This note is best used in describing only the other formats which are available in the library collection. Many items covered in this chapter are manufactured and issued in several types of formats, such as motion pictures and videorecordings on reel-to-reel tapes and on videocassettes of different standards. Although one can give information about the various formats in which an item is issued, for the library user, information about only those formats available in the collection is necessary. Information about the availability of various formats from the publisher is only confusing to the user who is trying to identify the holdings of a collection.

If a library collection contains the same item in different formats, the best way to describe each one is in a separate catalog entry. An alternate method, as explained in 7.5B1., is to provide a general descriptive phrase in the specific designator and more detail about each format available in your library in this note area, including all necessary details.

Physical description	3 videorecordings
Note	Available also as 1 videocassette (22 min.) : sd., col. ; 2 in. or 1 videocassette (22 min.) : sd., col. ; ½ in. or 1 videocassette (22 min.) : sd., col. ; ¾ in.
	Quadraplex, Beta, and U standards.

This method and multilevel description are confusing to the user and probably should be avoided. Again, a separate entry for each of the formats in your collection is preferable.

7.7B17. Summary

A brief overview, using phrases whenever possible, explaining the subject content, the scope, the point of view, and the nature of the visual and sound accompaniment is usually necessary, unless the content is evident from other parts of the description. Information in the summary can also include names of people or groups participating prominently in the film, in order to describe their relationship to the production. Significant technical or artistic attributes of the production can also be mentioned, if deemed important for the users.

A summary should avoid interpretation, evaluation, and prescription for use, although an implied audience can be noted. Promotional words or phrases which are found in the material and written by the publishers and distributors should also be avoided in the summary.

Summary notes

Summary: Shows painter Helen Frankenthaler creating a complete work; with friends and colleagues in her studio, at home, and at an exhibition of her work. Examines paintings and interviews colleagues and critics.

Summary: Animated characters made of sculpted Plasticine applied over glass create images of life after death. Without narration.

Summary: Interviewer with representative from IBM discuss jobs available to liberal arts graduates in large corporations.

Summary: Uses photomicrography and time-lapse sequences to show research technique of nuclear transplantation. Shows how nuclei are transplanted from donor body cells into activated eggs.

Summary: A documentary showing nurses working in hospitals, in independent practice, on strike and in support groups. Nurses discuss expectation vs. reality, nurses as a political force, collective bargaining, and professionalism.

7.7B20.   Copy being described
This note is useful particularly for tapes which have been recorded from a master copy, but differ from the original. If the differences are not covered in notes about the physical characteristics, they can be noted here. If portions of the production are missing or poorly recorded, this too can be noted.

7.8.   STANDARD NUMBER AND TERMS OF AVAILABILITY AREA

7.8D.   OPTIONAL ADDITION. TERMS OF AVAILABILITY
Any restrictions on the use of the material should be indicated. Also, items included in the catalog which are available to users through ways other than circulation from the collection should be noted.

Notes
Available to teaching staff only.

Free loan available from distributor.

EXAMPLES:
Descriptive Cataloging for Motion Pictures

Roll of thunder, hear my cry [motion picture] / Tomorrow Entertainment, Inc. — New York : Learning Corporation of
America, 1979.

3 film reels (110 min.) : sd., col. : 16 mm. + 1 study
guide.

Based on the book of the same title by Mildred D. Taylor.

Cast: Claudia McNeil, Janet McLachian, Robert Christian,
Roy Poole, Lark Ruffin, John Collum.

Credits: Producer, Jean Anne Moore ; director, Jack Smight ;
writer, Arthur Heinemann.

Summary: Set in the poverty-stricken South of 1933, tells
the story of a Black family's struggle to hold on to the land they
have owned for three generations.

I. Taylor, Mildred D. II. Tomorrow Entertainment
(Firm)

An adaption of a work of fiction into film entered under title. Note for an added
entry for author and same title on which film is based. Statement of responsibility
recorded as on item. Cast and credits taken from item.

Techniques of defense [motion picture]. — North Palm Beach,
Fla. : Athletic Institute, 1976.

1 film reel (20 min.) : sd., col. ; super 8 mm. — (Basketball ;
no. 4)

Summary: Assist in the teaching of basketball by focusing on
techniques of defense.

I. Athletic Institute. II. Series.

One film of a series which could have been cataloged as a set using series title.
Each part on separate reel and to be circulated separately. Physical description
sufficient because many types of equipment accommodate this format.

Dinky Hocker [motion picture] / Robert Guenette-Paul Asselin
  Productions. — New York : Learning Corporation of America,
  1979.

  1 film reel (30 min.) : sd., col. ; 16 mm. + 1 teacher's
guide.

  Based on the book entitled Dinkey Hocker shoots smack / M. E.
Kerr.

  Cast: Wendie Jo Sperber, June Lockhart.

  Credits: Director, Tom Blank ; film guide, John A. Matoian.

  Summary: Story of an adolescent girl who overeats and whose
mother is too involved with helping strangers to recognize her
daughter's needs.

  I. Kerr, M. E. Dinky Hocker shoots smack. II. Robert
Guenette-Paul Asselin Productions.

Title is the name of the main character. Responsibility assigned to production
company. Publisher and distributor are the same. Film for adolescents with guide
for teacher, but audience not stated on the item. Summary implies audience.

Water birds [motion picture]. — Mahwah, N.J. : Troll Associates,
  1972.

  1 film loop (4 min.) : si., col. ; super 8 mm. + 1 study
guide.

  Intended audience: Elementary through junior high grades.

  Summary: Various species of ducks, geese, and swans photographed in natural habitat.

Single concept film loop which fits several types of super 8 loop projectors. Short
films in cartridges are described as film loops, longer continuous loop films in
cartridges are described as cartridges. Audience on the item. Summary taken
from information on guide.

Hayward, C.O.
  The beginning [motion picture] : a film / by C.O. Hayward. —
[Santa Monica, Calif.] : Stephen Bosustow Productions,
1971.

  1 film reel (5 min.) : sd., col. ; 16 mm.

  Title on beginning frames: A Wiggleman tale.

  Intended audience: Elementary grades up.

  Summary: A parable with animated figures in which a butterfly
touches a person who is inspired to be different.

    I. Title. II. Title: A Wiggleman tale.

Main entry under person responsible, prominently named on title frames. Place
found in reference sources and not on film or container. The title of film, verified
in publisher's catalog, appears at the end of the film. Descriptive, introductory,
other title at the beginning.

Cosmic zoom [motion picture] / produced by the National Film
  Board of Canada. — New York : Contemporary Films,
  McGraw-Hill Films [distributor], 1970.

  1 film reel (8 min.) : sd., col. ; 16 mm.

  Based on the book Cosmic view by Keis Booke.

  Credits: Drawings, Eva Szasz ; animation camera, Raymond
Dumas, Wayne Trickett, James Wilson ; actuality camera, Tony
Ianelo.

  Intended audience: Elementary grades through college.

  Summary: Relates, in a wordless journey, the unseen microcosmic
universe within the human body to the limitless universe of space.
Uses camera zoom device.

    I. National Film Board of Canada. II. Booke, Keis.
Cosmic view.

Production company given statement of responsibility because of extent of
contribution. U.S. distributor given as appears on the item. Note for related
material in another format. Credits important because of the nature of the film
technique. Summary indicates film is non-narrated and mentions technique.

McLaren, Norman.
    Two bagatelles [motion piction] / by Norman McLaren and
Grant Monro. — [Montreal] : National Film Board of Canada,
1951.

    1 film reel (2 min., 22 sec.) : sd., col. ; 16 mm.

    Summary: Two examples of pixillation accompanied by different music.

    Contents: On the lawn — In the backyard.

       I. Monro, Grant. II. Title. III. Title: On the lawn. IV. Title: In the backyard.

Entry under the first named in statement of responsibility. Collective title for the two separate segments appears on the film, with filmmakers named as publisher. Film under 5 minutes also described with seconds. Summary describes technique. Contents note for separately titled parts. Added entries for other statement of responsibility and titles of parts.

———————

    Uncle Sam Magoo [motion picture] / United Productions of
       America. — Mt. Prospect, Ill. : Mar/Chuck Film Industries,
       [197-]

    1 film reel (28 min.) : sd., col. ; 16 mm.

    Credits: Music, Walter Scharf.

    Made in 1969.

    Longer version (52 min.) also issued.

    Summary: Cartoon character Mr. Magoo outlines America's history from the founding of the New World to the landing on the moon.

       I. United Productions of America.

Production company named in statement of responsibility. Slash in name of distributor not preceded or followed by a space. Two notes related to publication and date.

———————

EXAMPLES:
Descriptive Cataloging of Videorecordings

Younger, Irving.
   Everything you wanted to know about hearsay and were afraid
to ask. Part I [videorecording] / Lecturer, Irving Younger. —
[Chicago] : American Bar Association, 1976.

   1 videocassette (51 min.) : sd., col. ; ¾ in.

   Lecture presented at the American Bar Association Conference,
Section of Litigation in Atlanta, Georgia in 1976.

   U standard.

      I. American Bar Association Conference (1976 : Atlanta). II.
Title.

Entry under lecturer responsible for content. Place established from reference
sources. Note relating to statement of responsibility with information for added
entry. Standard for type of videorecording given in note. Title traced because it is
not main entry.

The New copyright law [videorecording] : issues and answers /
   Appalachian Education Satellite Project. — [Lexington, Ky. :
   University of Kentucky: distributed by AESP, 1978]

   2 videocassettes (90 min.) : sd., col. ; ¾ in.

   Includes segments of American Library Association teleconfer-
ence on copyright with Barbara Ringer, Register of Copyrights.

   U standard.

   Summary: A panel discussion about fair use, educational copy-
ing, and legal responsibilities of educators.

      I. Appalachian Education Satellite Project. II. American
Library Association.

Group named in statement of responsibility is also the distributor. Other
organization produced the item. First note relates to responsibility for part of
content. Second note to physical description. Added entry for organization
responsible for important segment.

The Light of experience [videorecording] / British Broadcasting
  Corporation. — New York : Time-Life Multimedia, 1971.

  1 videocassette (52 min.) : sd., col. ; ¾ in. + discussion guide. —
  (Civilization series ; no. 8)

  Issued in 1970 as a motion picture.

  U standard.

  Credits: Writer and narrator, Kenneth Clark.

  Summary: Surveys the development of Western civilization
  during the seventeenth century. Includes works of Dutch paint-
  ers and shows the change in thought that replaced divine authority
  with experience, experimentation, and observation.

        I. British Broadcasting Corp. II. Series.

Title entry because of mixed responsibility. Narrator and writer put in notes. U.S.
distributor named in publication, distribution area. Series given as it appears on
item and is traced as such. First note related to history and edition.

Non-verbal communication [videorecording]. — Santa Monica,
  Calif. : Salenger Educational Media, 1980.

  1 videocassette (14 min.) : sd., col. ; ¾ in.

  Made in 1979, a rev. version of videorecording first issued in
  1978 under the same title.

  U standard.

  With leader's guide, 20 worksheets and copy of The Silent
  messages (152 p.) by Albert Mehrabian.

  Summary: Psychologist Dr. Albert Mehrabian points out that
  an awareness of non-verbal messages enhances the ability to
  communicate.

        I. Mehrabian, Albert. II. Mehrabian, Albert. The silent
  messages. III. Salenger Educational Media.

Entry under title because of mixed responsibility. First note gives all information
about history and edition. Next note related to physical description.
Accompanying material omitted from physical description because of number of
items and need to give title of accompanying book. Added entries for personal
name as lecturer. Added entry for related accompanying author and book title.

VI
Description of Graphic Materials

8.0. GENERAL RULES

8.0A. SCOPE

This chapter covers the description of all types of two-dimensional materials, both opaque and transparent, some of which are intended for projection. Rules are appropriate for individual graphic items, graphic packages which contain many images intended to be viewed or displayed sequentially, such as the graphic images on a filmstrip, and sets of graphics published as a unit, such as a set of filmstrips. Films, microforms, and microscope slides are covered elsewhere, although slides on transparent film intended for projection are covered here. Maps which are published on a graphic format can be cataloged according to the rules in Chapter 3 or can be described in terms of the physical characteristics of the graphic format covered in this chapter, with additional information about the nature of the map content provided in notes. If a library has a separate map section or department, all maps, regardless of format, probably should be cataloged primarily as maps, with notes about the physical characteristics of the format. If maps are integrated into the general collection, the cataloger may decide to catalog the item as a graphic format according to this chapter, with notes about the characteristics of the map.

This chapter covers a large number of diverse types of materials, some of which are educational in content and some of which are not. For those not published for educational purposes or those produced locally, and perhaps not formally published, determining bibliographic information can be particularly difficult. Another problem for the cataloger is determining the most useful unit for the description of multipart items. For example, a group of slides or transparencies, either published or locally produced, could be described as individual items or as a group. The decision should be based on the intellectual unity of the material and on the needs of the users. Most graphic items should be cataloged as a unit, dictated by the way in which they are published and packaged. For example, a set of four or five filmstrips should usually be handled as a unit. Likewise, a slide presentation with a theme or subject focus should also be cataloged as a unit.

Graphic materials accompanied by sound, such as sound filmstrips and slide-tape presentations, where the sound is intended to be used in the presentation of the material as narrative and/or musical accompaniment for the visuals, should be cataloged according to the rules in this chapter. Only when graphics packaged with sound are intended to be viewed independently and when the sound packaged with the graphics is intended to be used separately from the graphic material should the material be cataloged as a kit. See the definition of "kit" in the *AACR 2* Glossary. Sound may or may not be integral, that is, physically inseparable from the graphic. If accompanying sound is necessary or a complement to the graphic material, the material is considered to be a graphic. The assumption is that the intellectual burden of the content is contained in the graphic with accompanying information or artistic enhancement presented in the sound accompaniment.

The Prints and Photographs Division of the Library of Congress has published a preliminary draft of "Rules for Cataloging Graphic Materials" intended to "supply the additional guidance necessary to catalog original, historical, and archival graphic materials." The final draft, scheduled to appear in 1982, will be a modification and expansion of the rules which appear in Chapter 8 of *AACR 2*. Although these rules attempt to be "consistent with both the principles of museum/archives description of graphic materials the structure and philosophy of the Anglo-American cataloging rules," according to the cover letter accompanying the draft from LC, there are many significant differences in even basic rules, such as the application of the standard GMDs. LC's list is different from the list appearing in *AACR 2*. The numbering structure of the rules is not compatible with *AACR 2*, and the catalog record resulting from application of these rules is quite different in many respects. A library with a sizeable special collection of archival graphic materials may want to consider application of these rules. Libraries which integrate the bibliographic records for graphics with those of other materials will probably want to follow *AACR 2* when LC's rules differ from the *AACR 2* rules. The final draft of these rules will contain a glossary and other helpful information which will be of use to any cataloger of graphic materials.

8.0B. SOURCES OF INFORMATION

8.0B1. Chief source of information
The chief source which is the preferred source for most descriptive areas is the item itself, including its labels and a container which are integral parts of the item, that is, physically inseparable from it. The chief source for a multipart item, however, is a container which is not integral, if it provides a collective title and the items do not. If information is not available from the chief source which is the item or the integral container, it can be taken from:

- a container which is not integral
- accompanying material
- any other sources.

All of the parts of a multipart graphic item can contribute information as a chief source. In a sound filmstrip set, title frames from each of several filmstrips which contain collective title information can be considered. Lacking a collective title on the filmstrips, the chief source for title information could be the container which is not integral or accompanying material such as a teacher's guide.

8.0B2. Prescribed sources of information
For each area of description there are given prescribed source(s) from which the information can be taken without bracketing it in the description. Examine the chief source(s) and extract from the chief source(s) information for the following areas:

Area 1. Title and statement of responsibility
    2. Edition
    4. Publication, distribution, etc.
    6. Series

If information is not found in the item itself as the chief source, next examine the container and extract information for the following areas:

Area 1. Title and statement of responsibility
    2. Edition
    3. Publication, distribution, etc.
    6. Series

If information is not found in the item or on the container, examine the accompanying material and extract information for the following areas:

Area 2. Edition
    4. Publication, distribution, etc.
    6. Series

Information taken from sources other than those indicated for each area must be bracketed.

If information is not found in any of the above sources, take from any information source without bracketing it for the following areas:

Area 5. Physical description
    7. Notes
    8. Standard number and terms of availability

Any information required by the chosen level of description can be taken from any source if the information is bracketed. Prefer the prescribed sources in the order given in case of conflicting information found on the various sources.

In some cases, the accompanying material is the only unifying element for a graphic production and may contain the most accurate information relating to the production as a whole. Parts of multipart graphic items may be published or produced at different times or may be produced by different groups or individuals. The items may be brought together as a finished package only when the accompanying material is published. In these cases, the accompanying material, and not the container, is the unifying element and should be used as the chief source.

8.1. TITLE AND STATEMENT OF RESPONSIBILITY AREA

8.1B. TITLE PROPER

Record the title proper as instructed in 1.1B. The prescribed sources of information are the item itself and an integral container, or the container or other part which provides a collective title for a multipart item. Lacking information on the chief source(s), bracket information taken from other sources. The cataloger can supply a title for a single graphic item or a collection of graphic items according to 1.1B7.

Bibliographic information from the item

Title frame **First filmstrip of** **set**	Washington, D. C. The CITY FREEDOM BUILT

Container	Washington five filmstrip adventures in full color and sound NATIONAL GEOGRAPHIC SOCIETY Encyclopaedia Britannica Educational Corporation

Title taken from
container
	Washington [filmstrip] / National Geographic
	    Society. — [Chicago] : Encyclopaedia
	    Britannica Educational Corp., c1968.

Supplied title	[Beethoven listening to a cassette player] [transparency]. —

Other title information
following GMD
	Perspectives and challenges [filmstrip] : a
	    national program for library and information
	    services / presented by the National Commis-
	    sion on Library and Information Science ;
	    [made by] Image Innovations. —

Parallel title **following GMD**	The Bullfrog [transparency] = Rana catesbiana. —

8.1C1. Optional addition. General material designation
Follow the title proper with a GMD chosen from the following list, and give the term in the singular.

art original	picture
chart	slide
filmstrip	technical drawing
flash card	transparency

The term "picture" is to be used when a graphic item does not fit into one of the other categories. The use of the generic term in the GMD will be explained further in the specific designation of the physical description in 8.5B1. and in the notes.

8.1F. STATEMENTS OF RESPONSIBILITY

Statements of responsibility are recorded as instructed in 1.1F. They should be recorded only if appearing prominently in the chief source(s) of information. In most cases, this would exclude information found only in accompanying material, unless it is the unifying element and would exclude information found in sources outside the item. A short word or phrase explaining the relationship between the title and statement of responsibility, preferably one appearing on the item, can be added to the statement of responsibility.

Title frame

The Island of the Skog
story and pictures by
Steven Kellogg

Filmstrip copyright c. 1976 Weston Woods Studios, Inc.

(On side of filmstrip "Kellogg – The Island of the Skog Dial.")

(This is a photograph of the cover of the book. The filmstrip illustrations are copies of the pictures in the book.)

Statement of responsibility with explanatory phrase	Kellogg, Steven. The Island of the Skog [filmstrip] / story and pictures by Steven Kellogg. —
Two statements with explanatory phrase	Family [filmstrip] / Herbert and Judith Klinger ; made by Educational Designs, Inc. —

8.1G. ITEMS WITHOUT A COLLECTIVE TITLE

For multipart graphic items with no collective title and for which a supplied title is appropriate because of unity of the items in the collection, supply a title from accompanying material or outside sources.

Supplied collective title from publisher's catalog

[The Cat in famous paintings] [slide]. —

Supplied title and statement of responsibility from unifying element, the booklet

[The American Revolution] [picture] / People's Bicentennial Commission. —

(A group of posters of various sizes for display accompanied by booklet.)

For multipart items containing a large number of diverse parts, the cataloger can record titles of individual parts as instructed in 1.1G.

8.2. EDITION AREA

8.2B. EDITION STATEMENT
Use the rules in 1.2B. to record information about the edition. The optional addition, suggested in 8.2B3., of a statement in brackets concerning the edition of a graphic item which lacks a statement on the item will not be done by LC and probably would be better given in a note relating to the edition area under 8.7B7. (notes relating to edition and history). Packaging of graphic materials in different combinations is common practice with nonprint publishers. These facts are often complicated and can be more fully explained in notes than in the body of the description. When a part of a multipart item, such as one filmstrip in a set of four, has been published separately, perhaps under a separate or even different title, this information can be given in a note. Added entries can also be based on this information.

Edition information in note

Reality orientation [filmstrip]. — Garden Grove, Calif. : Trainex Corp., 1977.

Edited from the 1975 American Hospital Association slide set entitled This way to reality.

8.4. PUBLICATION, DISTRIBUTION, ETC., AREA

8.4A2. Art originals, unpublished photographs, etc.
Locally produced graphics or those which are not formally published and made available for mass distribution are treated differently from published material in this area. Because they are unavailable from a publisher, distributor, or manufacturer, the place of publication, distribution, or manufacture is not given. No name is given, and only the date associated with the making of the item appears in this area. If some of this information is known, even though the item which is locally produced is not available from the source, the information can be given in a note. The information should be given when it is known, because materials produced without initial, formal publication often are published later by the organization or individual responsible for local production.

Local production without place, publication elements information in note

[8 mm. motion picture equipment] [transparency] . — [1974]

Made by the Media Lab, College of Library Science, University of Kentucky.

8.4A3. Collections of graphic materials
Collections of materials, without unifying accompanying material which may or may not have a collective title, require only the inclusive dates of the materials in this area. Individual items may or may not have been formally published by one or a number of different publishers.

Untitled collection; title supplied

[The Artic] [picture]. — [S.1.] : Alaska Airlines,
[196?-1970]

(Three posters published by the same organization.)

8.4B. GENERAL RULE

Instructions regarding the information provided in this area are found in
1.4B. In describing a graphic item which is a reproduction of another graphic or
of an item in another format, such as a photograph of a three-dimensional item,
give the descriptive details of the reproduction in this area. Information about the
original, if it appears on the item or in accompanying material, can be given in a
note under 8.7B7., 8.7B8., or 8.7B9.

Reproduction of photo in another format

Join the midnight sun set in Alaska [picture] / photograph by
Frank Whaley. — [S.1.] : /Air Alaska, c1970.

1 poster : col. ; 90 x 60 cm.

Copy of a time-lapse photograph of the Artic sun taken
between 11:00 A. M. and 1:00 A. M.

If an item has more than one place of publication, distribution, etc. or more
than one publisher, distributor, or manufacturer named, describe it in terms of
the first named place and the corresponding publisher, distributor, etc. If the first
named is only a distributor or releasing agent, add the name of the publisher
according to rule 1.4B8. This rule also requires the recording of the place and
name of principal publisher, if one is indicated by the layout. It is possible to have
several names associated with each type of function. In each category, publisher,
distributor, etc., the first named and any subsequent agency named prominently
should be recorded.

The prescribed sources of information for this area include the chief source,
the container, and accompanying material. Several places and names are likely to
be included in these sources. According to these rules, the first named and the
principal publisher should be included in this area. Names are often given in
different forms in the various sources of information for graphics. Prefer the
form of the name found in the prescribed sources in the order listed above in
8.0B2. Generally, the chief source would be the item itself, including labels, or an
integral container; the container would be next, followed by accompanying
material.

8.4E. OPTIONAL ADDITION. STATEMENT OF FUNCTION OF PUBLISHER, DISTRIBUTOR, ETC.

8.4E1.

A word or phrase designating the function of those named in this area can
optionally be added to the name or names. This option should be used in cases
where a phrase, indicating the function, is not available from the item, is not

recorded, or in cases where the function is not clear from the context of the information given in the body of the entry. The words or phrases to be used as indicated in 1.4E1. are:

distributor   producer
publisher   production company

See the *AACR 2* Glossary for a definition of "producer" and "production company."

Statement of function

> Diagnosis and treatment planning in endodontics [slide] : pulpal pathosis / Medical University of South Carolina, College of Dental Medicine, Department of Endodontics. — Charleston, S.C. : The Dept. ; Washington : National Audiovisual Center [distributor], 1978.

8.5. PHYSICAL DESCRIPTION AREA

8.5B. EXTENT OF ITEM (INCLUDING SPECIFIC MATERIAL DESIGNATION)

The total number of physical units of the graphic being described, followed by a specific designator, are the first two elements in this area. The list of specific designators found in 8.5B1. includes some generic designators and some terms which are not GMDs. A term can be chosen from this list, or optionally, a more specific term can be used as a specific designator. The most specific term covering all of the graphics included in a multipart item should be used here. The GMD must be chosen from those standard terms found in 1.1C1., but a great variety of terms can be used here. The various specific material designations will be apportioned among the GMDs by the Library of Congress as follows:

Chart	Picture	Slide
Chart	Art print	Slide
Flip chart	Art reproduction	Stereograph
Wall chart	Photograph	Technical drawing
Filmstrip	Picture	Technical drawing
Filmslip	Postcard	Transparency
Filmstrip	Poster	Transparency
Flashcard	Radiograph	
Flash card	Study print	

If they apply, all of the rules in 8.5B. should be considered for all of the graphic formats.

8.5C. OTHER PHYSICAL DETAILS

Because this chapter covers many different types of graphics having dissimilar details, rules are given alphabetically for the specific designators listed. If a designator which is more specific than those listed is used, follow the rules for recording other physical details for the general type of material being cataloged.

The intended use of the item is one factor in determining the specific designator. For example, a poster, which would be assigned the generic term "picture" in the GMD, may be a reproduction of a photograph. Its intended use as a poster would indicate that it be assigned this term in the specific designator. Study prints may contain reproductions of art originals, but their use would determine the specific designator "study print." Many graphics will be described as [picture] in the GMD with another term appearing in the specific designator.

The terms used in describing other physical details are not standardized. They are best taken from information on the item itself or from accompanying material.

8.5C4. Filmstrips and filmslips

Sound is indicated with other physical details only when it is integral, in other words, recorded on the film itself. These filmstrips are rare and not represented in most library collections. In almost all cases, sound accompanying filmstrips will be described as accompanying material and not described here.

8.5C12. Slides

Only one or two systems exist to record and playback sound which is integral to slides, that is, sound recorded on the slide mount. Because the several systems available to record sound on slides are not interchangable, the name of the system should be given as other physical details.

8.5D. DIMENSIONS

Instructions for giving the height and width of graphics, with the exception of filmstrips, filmslips, and stereographs, are given in 8.5D1. and other rules in 8.5D. Filmstrips are described in terms of width, which is usually 35mm. Dimensions for slides are given only if they are different from the standard 2x2-inch slides. Different types of cameras and film produce standard slides with different size apertures for the visual. All of the slides, however, can be viewed with equipment which projects or allows for the viewing of transparencies mounted in a standard size mount. Other sizes include 1-3/16x1-3/16-inch slides produced with 110 film, 2¼x2¼-inch slides produced with 120 or 620 film, and 3¼x4-inch lantern slides. These sizes must be given in metric measure.

8.5E. ACCOMPANYING MATERIAL

When graphic material is accompanied by sound and/or textual material, 8.5E1. provides that the name of the material, i.e., a specific designator or other name of the material, be recorded at the end of the physical description preceded by a " + ." For textual material, the name of the type of item, not the title, is recorded from the item. Booklets, study guides, scripts, and students' manuals are often included and named as such. Sound accompaniments often included are sound discs and cassettes. Optionally, the cataloger can record the physical description of this accompanying material. This does not include integral sound, physically inseparable from the item which is described as "other physical details" as part of the physical description of the graphic itself. The majority of material to be used with a graphic item is not integral and will be covered by this rule.

The rule for the four methods of recording information about accompanying material is 1.5E1. The methods provide for recording information about accompanying material:

a. in a separate entry
b. in a multilevel description according to Chapter 13
c. in a note according to 1.7B11. and 8.7B11.
d. at the end of the physical description.

According to 8.5E1., the name of the material should be given at the end of the physical description. The option discussed in 1.5E1., method d. provides the opportunity to include further description of accompanying material in the physical description. Each of these methods is viable, but method d. is most appropriate for graphic packages.

A separate entry for each part of a package, suggested in method a., is desirable and necessary only when the parts are separated, cataloged separately, classified differently, and housed separately. Multilevel description is complicated for the cataloger and confusing to the user. A combination of methods c. and d. produce a unified record for the item and can clearly present all of the information needed by the user. Most graphic materials are accompanied by only one or two other types of material. Each of these can be included in the physical description each preceded by a " + ." Either one or both of these materials can be described in the physical description in terms of a statement of extent, other physical details, and dimensions. The mnemonic numbering structure allows the cataloger to consult the appropriate chapter for the type of format of the accompanying material, for extent under .5B., for the other physical details under .5C., and for dimensions under .5D. To describe a sound recording which accompanies graphic material, the cataloger would first apply the rules for the graphic in the physical description and then apply the rules for physical description of sound recordings in 6.5. for the sound accompaniment.

Because playback of the material requires equipment, a complete description of the accompanying sound in the physical decription is useful. Also, because the duration of the sound accompaniment determines the duration of the production, providing this information in the expanded description of the accompanying material is desirable. If several types of accompanying materials are included with graphic items, a combination of complete descriptions for those requiring equipment and a limited description for those not requiring equipment provides a good solution. Describe an accompanying sound recording in detail; describe a booklet in notes. Also, notes related to the content of the accompanying material but not descriptive of the physical characteristics of the material can be included in the notes. The physical description of accompanying material is enclosed in parentheses. The punctuation is somewhat different from that used when the material is described as a separate item.

Physical description

Single graphic items

1 filmstrip (48 fr.) : col. ; 35 mm.

1 art original : woodcut on paper ; 20 x 42 cm.

1 transparency : col. ; 19 x 24 cm.

1 technical drawing : b&w ; 60 x 40 cm.

Multipart items without accompanying material

4 filmstrips (ca. 45 fr. ea.) : b&w ; 35 mm.

2 posters : col. ; 53 x 36 cm.

80 slides : col.

Multipart items with accompanying material without optional physical description

4 filmstrips : col. ; 35 mm. + 1 sound disc.

4 filmstrips : col. ; 35 mm. + 4 sound cassettes + 1 teacher's guide.

120 slides : col. + 2 sound cassettes + 2 sound discs + 1 script.

Multipart items with accompanying material with optional physical description

5 filmstrips : col. ; 35 mm. + 5 sound discs (ca. 90 min. : 33⅓ rpm, mono. ; 12 in.) + 1 teacher's guide.

6 filmstrips : col. ; 35 mm. + 3 sound cassettes (86 min. : 1⅞ ips, 2 track, mono.) + 1 study guide.

160 slides : col. + 2 sound cassettes (30 min. : 1⅞ ips, 2 track, mono.)

8.6. SERIES AREA

In determining series relationships, catalogers should be careful to follow the definition offered by *AACR 2*. Characteristics of a true series include items:

- related and bearing their own title as well as a collective title
- which may or may not be numbered within the series
- which are issued in sequence.

Publishers of nonprint items often use pseudo-series as a marketing devise. A single publication may be listed as part of several groupings by a publisher in order to list the item in several areas of a buyer's interest. Unless the series fits the definition above, the series should not be recorded here.

Series as final element of physical description

1 filmstrip (53 fr.) : col. ; 35 mm. + 1 sound cassette (9 min. : 1⅞ ips, 2 track, mono.). — (Let's learn the basics)

(One filmstrip of a set of 5 cataloged separately. Collective title of the set is recorded as series title.)

6 filmstrips : col. ; 35 mm. + 3 sound cassettes (86 min. : 1⅞ ips, 2 track, mono.) + 1 teacher's guide. — (SRA/CBS News filmstrip series)

(Series of filmstrip sets, unnumbered.)

---

8 study prints : col. ; 33 x 46 cm. + 1 sound disc. — (Basic science series ; PSSP-100)

(Series which is numbered.)

---

1 filmstrip (87 fr.) : col. ; 35 mm. + 1 sound cassette + 1 program guide + 1 overview guide. — (Optics ; pt. 4) (Physics: fundamental concepts)

(One filmstrip of a set cataloged separately with set given as first series, series made up of several sets given as second series statement.)

8.7. NOTE AREA

8.7B3. Source of title proper

When a title proper is chosen from a source of information other than the chief source or is supplied by the cataloger, note the source of the information. A unifying part, such as accompanying material or a container which is not integral, will often be the best source for title information; for example:

Source notes

Title taken from study guide.

Title supplied from publisher's catalog.

Title supplied from data sheet.
(Data sheet supplied to cataloging agency by publisher.)

8.7B4. Variations in title

Often, the title on a graphic package varies from one source to another. Note these variations if they are significant and if a user is likely to identify the item by a title other than that used as the title proper.

Title proper	American history I [flash card] : discovery to Civil War. —

Variation in title note	Title on box top: American history I : summary cards.

8.7B6. Statements of responsibility
Names associated with the content and production of graphic items may not appear prominently in the chief source and therefore would not be named in the statement of responsibility in the body of the entry. These names can be recorded in notes. No specific directions are given for recording cast and credits, but individuals and groups can be named in informal notes.

Credit notes

Writer, Carol Deegan ; program guide, Marion Wilson ; photo editor, Miriam Weidig ; project editor, Sally Paris.

(Some names from filmstrip frames, some names from program guide.)

Script and picture research, Patricia Greene ; visual editor, Beatrice Fuhring ; editor, Gladys Carter.
Narrator, Barrett Clark ; voices, Doug Mathewson, Gloria Rascoe, Sonny Sharrock.

Producer, David S. Boyer.

(From end frame of filmstrip.)

Consultant, Lu Ouida Vinson, American Library Association.

(From accompanying material.)

Prepared by Helen R. Hollis with assistance from James M. Weaver.
Consultant, Mark Lindley ; bibliography, Anne Melton Kimzey.

(From accompanying materials, persons in organization not named in statement of responsibility.)

8.7B7. Edition and history
Names and titles associated with a work in another format on which a graphic item is based or to which it is related can be noted here.

Notes on edition and history

Picture from Charles Kuralt's On the road series filmed in 1976.

(Filmstrip using stills from production in another format.)

Original in The Louvre, Paris.

Detail of original painting in Folger Library.

A reissue of an item, particularly as part of a different set or series, should be noted with any title change or change of content.

8.7B10. Physical description

Any important details which are not given in the physical description area for the graphic items themselves can be given in these notes. Characteristics which determine the method of viewing should be included.

Notes relating to graphic item

Mounted and framed, measures 73 x 59 cm. framed.

(Art reproduction.)

In plastic mounts, 23 x 30 cm. in container, 24 x 32 x 4 cm.

(Transparency set.)

In two carousel trays.

(Slides.)

Glass mounted.

(Slides.)

In container 32 x 43 x 4 cm.

(Filmstrip with discs.)

8.7B11. Accompanying material
Notes about accompanying materials are needed when using descriptive methods c. and d. in rule 1.5E1. Using method c., only the extent of the item for accompanying material is given in the physical description, and other physical details and dimensions can be included here. When using method d., details of some accompanying materials may be included in the physical description, and others can be given in this area in the notes.

Notes relating to accompanying material

Sound cassette with automatic advance.

Sound cassette side 1 with automatic advance, side 2 without signal.

Sound cassette side 1 with automatic advance, side 2 with audible advance signal.

Sound disc side 1 with automatic advance, side 2 with audible advance signal.

For use with Viewmaster projector.

Sound cassette (30 min. : 1⅞ ips, 2 track, mono.)

Sound disc (12 min. : 45 rpm, mono. ; 7 in.)

Teacher's guide (12 p. : col. ; 18 cm.)

Study guide on cover of sound disc.

Instructions for use on container.

8.7B14. Audience
If an intended audience is identified by the publisher or those responsible for content, this can be noted. A descriptive phrase used on the item or in a publisher's catalog is preferable. This information can be oriented toward age or grade of users, and/or special types of users. If no such information is available on the item or in literature associated with the item, the purpose of the item is better incorporated into the summary. Although schools may prefer to give grade level indications for instructional materials, unless the publisher indicates appropriate levels, assigning audience level by the cataloger may limit the potential use of the material and should be avoided.

Notes

Intended audience: Primary grades.

Intended audience: For parents of handicapped children.

Intended audience: For paralegal personnel.

8.7B16. Other formats available
Because this note, which is intended to describe other forms of the item, can easily be overlooked by the user, a separate entry in the catalog for each form of the item which is in the library's collection is preferable to giving the information here. This note should not be used for information about other formats available outside the collection.

Graphic items with sound accompaniment are often published with options for purchase of the format of sound accompaniment. For example, slide sets come with disc or cassette, sound filmstrip sets offer the same option. Also, there are often options in the sound accompaniment for manual and/or automatic advance signals or for sound without any signals. The library which uses cataloging information from the Library of Congress should be aware that LC provides a collation or physical description and notes relating to all of the optional, accompanying sound offered by the publisher. Each library should provide a physical description and notes appropriate to the item in hand and be careful to edit any cataloging information from LC or other sources accordingly. Again, this method is confusing to the user, a separate catalog entry for each available format is preferable.

If this note is used, it should indicate that an alternative format is available in the collection and should give sufficient detail about the nature of the other format.

Note on other format available for slides accompanied by sound

Also available as 1 filmstrip (45 fr.) : col. ; 35 mm. + 1 sound cassette (15 min. : 1⅞ ips, 2 track, mono.). Sound accompaniment with manual or automatic advance signals. Cassette side 1 without signal, side 2 inaudible signal for automatic advance.

Note on other available format for filmstrip and disc

Also available with sound cassette (30 min. : 1⅞ ips, 2 track, mono.) with side 1 audible signal and side 2 inaudible advance signal.

8.7B17. Summary

Giving a formal note, headed by the word "Summary," and followed by a colon enables the user to easily locate the information on the catalog record. The note should be brief, using phrases whenever possible. The information should describe what the user will see and experience. It should not be evaluative and should avoid interpretation. The summary should enable the user to gain a general idea of the subject content, the scope of the content, and the point of view of the presentation. Significant technical or artistic attributes can also be mentioned, but without evaluation. The nature of the visual treatment and the type of sound can be mentioned as well. Although contents notes are often descriptive of the topics covered, a summary can provide information about the way in which the format addresses the topic.

Summary notes

Sound filmstrip

Summary: Three cartoon episodes conceived and narrated by Art Buchwald, English comedians Flanders and Swann, and Bill Cosby demonstrate typical struggles between adolescents and their parents.

Postcard

Summary: Shows front and side view of the building.

Chart

Summary: Illustrates 12 cell types with 40 labels.

Graphics package

Summary: Items divided into 12 displays with visuals and captions for each.

Flash cards

Summary: Each card contains a topic heading and questions on one side and answers on the other.

Sound slide set

Summary: Uses art, music, and photography to discuss need for planning the future with technology. Illustrates ways technology may affect the family, religion, education, the arts, and the environment.

8.7B18.   Contents notes

Contents notes are necessary for multipart graphics with individually titled parts. Each named part can include title and statement of responsibility if needed.

Although sound accompaniment may determine the duration of a graphic presentation, the length of the presentation is described in terms of the graphic component. For example, this would include the number of frames in a filmstrip or the number of slides in a presentation. If this information is not sufficient to indicate the duration, a note about the length of the sound accompaniment can be included under 8.7B11. when the accompanying material is not described in detail in the physical description.

Contents notes

Filmstrip set

Contents: Introducing the library (43 fr.) — Using the card catalog (45 fr.) — Using reference works (43 fr.) — Reports and research (44 fr.)

Slide set

Contents: Part I (76 slides) — Part II (80 slides)

Slides set with collective title

Contents: Peasants at supper / Louis LeNain — Feasts of the bean / Jordeans — Graham Children / Hogarth — etc.

(The cataloger would continue to list all of the individual titles included in the set if important to users of the collection.)

8.7B19. Numbers

Few graphic materials will be assigned ISBNs or ISSNs. However, other numbers, usually assigned by the publisher within their ordering system, should be recorded. Multipart items will often carry numbers for the individual parts as well as for the package. Individual numbers should always be recorded when a package number is not assigned. If the package has a number, the numbers of individual parts are not as necessary, but are nevertheless, useful. Numbers recorded in the note should be associated with the part(s) to which they refer.

Number notes

Sound filmstrip set

> Filmstrip: 174.
> Sound cassette: 174 C.

Study prints with disc

> Picture story study prints: SP104.
> Sound disc: TSP 104 RR.

Postcard

> "119528"

Single filmstrip in set cataloged separately

> Filmstrip no. 14166.

Sound slide set

> 258.

Chart assigned ISBN

> ISBN 0-385-14323-0.

(Examples begin on page 130)

EXAMPLES:
Descriptive Cataloging for Graphics

Art original

Hassam, Childe.
[Street corner with carriage and crowd] [art original] / Childe
Hassam. — 1888.

1 art original : oil on cigar box cover ; 20 x 30 cm.

Size when framed: 41 x 34 cm.

University of Kentucky property no.: B730339
Accession no.: 79.28.

An original oil with supplied title. Object is signed. Framed size given because it differs significantly from object. Numbers needed for identification within collection.

Art print

Cezanne, Paul.
The blue vase [picture] / by Paul Cezanne. — [New York] :
Abrams, [19--]

1 art print : col. ; 63 x 49 cm.

Original in the Louvre Museum, Paris.

I. Title.

A reproduction of an art work entered under artist of original. Place determined from reference sources. Date undeterminable. Exact process for reproducing the item unknown.

Chart

Periodic chart of the elements [chart]. — Rev. ed. — Los
Angeles : Chemical Services, 1978, c1969.

1 chart : double sides, b&w ; 22 x 28 cm.

Contents: Side 1. Chart of the elements based on carbon-12 —
Side 2. Chemical valence and planetary electrons / I. Shapiro.

Lacking a statement of responsibility for whole item, entry under title. Edition statement found on item. Type not specific, resulting in use of term "chart," only in specific designator. Contents note made for titled parts.

Single filmstrip with sound accompaniment

> Perspectives and challenges [filmstrip] : a national program for library and information services / presented by the National Commission on Libraries and Information Science ;·[made by] Image Innovations. — Washington, D.C. : The Commission, 1978.
>
> 1 filmstrip (156 fr.) : col. ; 35 mm. + 1 sound cassette (25 min. : 1⅞ ips, 2 track, mono.) + 1 guide.
>
> Sound accompaniment for manual or automatic operation.
> Summary: Structured around library professionals at Statewide Library Planning Committee meeting. Presents aspects of proposed national program of NCLIS.
>
> I. United States. National Commission on Libraries and Information Science.

Although lengthy, entire title proper given and not abridged. Statement of responsibility appears prominently on the item. Statement showing relationship of production company does not appear in chief source. Shortened form of the name of the publisher already given in entry. Two types of accompanying material, one requiring equipment, described in detail. Accompanying print material not described in detail.

(Examples continue on page 132)

Filmstrip set

Bibliographic information on item

Box container
front

WASHINGTON
Five Filmstrip Adventures in full color and sound
  NATIONAL GEOGRAPHIC SOCIETY
Encyclopaedia Britannica Educational Corporation

Title frames
first filmstrip

Washington, D. C.
The City Freedom Built

The National Geographic Society
and the
Encyclopaedia Britannica Educational Corporation
present

---

from the worldwide resources
of the National Geographic

The City Freedom Built
c 1968 by the National Geographic Society and
Encyclopaedia Britannica Educational Corporation

First filmstrip
end frames

The City Freedom Built
Producer Davis S. Boyer
An educational service from
The National Geographic Society
School Services Division
Ralph Gray, Chief

Filmstrip set

Washington [filmstrip] / National Geographic Society. — [Chicago] : Encyclopaedia Britannica Educational Corp., c1968.

5 filmstrips : col. ; 35 mm. + 5 sound discs (33⅓ rpm, mono. ; 12 in.)

Sound accompaniment contains advance signals for manual and automatic operation.
Each disc cover contains script.
Contents: The city freedom built (83 fr.) — The United States Capitol (94 fr.) — The White House (84 fr.) — The Supreme Court (95 fr.) — Shrines and monuments (88 fr.).

6420.

I. National Geographic Society.

Entry under title. Firm responsibility does not qualify for corporate entry under 21.1B. Statement of responsibility given because of typography on box combined with statement on end frames. Place determined from reference sources. In physical description, accompanying material described. Duration omitted because difficult to determine. Number of frames, indicated in contents notes, gives indication of length of production. Note on sound implies type of equipment needed. No summary necessary because of information in contents note, although could be given. In the absence of a standard number, the number assigned to the item by the publisher is given as the last note according to 8.7B19.

An American sampler [filmstrip] / produced by CBS News and Joshua Tree Productions. — Chicago : Science Research Associates, c1974.

6 filmstrips : col. ; 35 mm. + 3 sound cassettes (86 min. : 1⅞ ips, 2 track, mono.) + teacher's guide. — SRA/CBS News filmstrip series)

Based on Charles Kuralt's On the road series for CBS News.
Narrator: Charles Kuralt.
Sound cassettes with audible signals.
Intended audience: Intermediate and secondary grades.
Summary: An anthology of human interest stories and a structured examination of the country's life styles.
Contents: America : variety and individualism (79 fr.) — America celebrates tradition (68 fr.) — America : changing and unchanged (97 fr.) — Americans and their land (70 fr.) — America on the go (72 fr.) — Americans and a job well done (63 fr.).
No. 3-11000.
I. Kuralt, Charles. II. CBS News. III. Science Research Associates. IV. Series.

Collective title on container and filmstrips. Statement of responsibility also on both. Science Research Associates is both publisher and distributor.

Accompanying material described in detail. Unnumbered series recorded. First two notes relate to the statement of responsibility. Nature of the sound determined by listening to them, lacking the information on the cassettes themselves or in the guide. Summary taken from the guide. Contents listed with number of frames for each. If all the same length, this could have been recorded in the physical description. Added entries for all information which might be used by library patron in locating item. A well-known publisher can be listed here.

Flash card set

> Steiner, Wilfred J.
>   American history I [flash card] : discovery to Civil War / by Wilfred J. Steiner. — Springfield, Ohio : Visual Education Association, [197-?]
>
>   1000 flash cards : col. ; 4 x 9 cm. + 1 booklet.
>
>   Intended audience: High school and college.
>   Booklet contains "Table of contents," "Alphabetical index," "Major topic headings."
>   Summary: Side 1 of each card contains a topic heading and one or more questions. Side 2 contains the answers.
>
>   VE507.
>
>   I. Title.

Main entry under author prominently named. Number included as part of title proper. GMD preceding the other title information. Decade certain because of information appearing on the cards; no other date information on the item. Intended audience on the item as given. Note on accompanying material. Summary needed. Publisher's number included as the last note.

Flip chart

> Campbell, Anneke.
>   Your pregnancy year [chart] : a day-by-day guide to pregnancy and birth / by Anneke Campbell. — 1st ed. — Garden City, N.Y. : Doubleday, c1979.
>
>   1 flip chart (13 sheets) : col. ; 28 x 41 cm.
>
>   Summary: On the left of each page is a description of progress of pregnancy. On the right, in calendar, is space for user's pregnancy record.
>
>   ISBN 0-385-14323-0.
>
>   I. Title.

Entry under person responsible prominently named on item. Other title information follows GMD. Number of sheets indicated in physical description. Summary needed. Published by company which assigned item a book number which is recorded.

Postcard

>Law Building, University of Kentucky, Lexington [picture]. — Louisville, Ky. : Postal Color Corp., [196-]
>
>1 postcard : col. ; 9 x 14 cm.
>
>Summary: Front view of building completed in 1965.
>
>119528.

Title taken from item. Decade certain. Summary useful. Publisher's number included as the last note.

Poster

>Alpha.
>Photo of monkey jungle, Miami, Fla. [picture] / by Alpha. — Niles, Ill. : Argus Communications, c1976.
>
>1 poster : col. ; 53 x 36 cm.
>
>Summary: An orangutan pointing with caption, "Don't follow me — I'm lost."
>
>Poster 2333.

Title and statement of responsibility taken from information on back of poster. The caption is not the title. The graphic content is basis of description.

(Examples continue on page 136)

Poster display package

[The American Revolution] [picture] / People's Bicentennial
Commission. — Washington : The Commission, [1976?]

76 posters : b&w ; 22 x 28 cm. + 1 booklet.

Booklet, entitled The patriot's handbook : a syllabus and study
guide to the American Revolution, includes a bibliography following each of its 14 sections.

Summary: Fourteen poster displays depicting the American
Revolution through illustrations, captions, and text.

I. People's Bicentennial Commission.

Package lacks a collective title which is supplied. Statement of responsibility
found prominently on booklet, the unifying element. Shortened form of
publisher's name already given in entry. Probable date for material published by
group formed to celebrate bicentennial. Added entry for the group responsible.

Slide set with sound accompaniment

How to live with your parents and survive [slide]. — White Plains,
N.Y. : The Center for Humanities, c1975.

80 slides : col. + 1 sound disc + 2 sound cassettes + 1 teacher's
guide.

Duration of same sound accompaniment in 3 forms is 14 min.
Disc side 1 with audible signal, side 2 without signal.
1 cassette side 1 with audible signal, side 2 without signal.
1 cassette side 1 with audible signal, side 2 with inadible
signal.
Guide contains script, credits, and references.

Summary: Three cartoon episodes conceived and narrated by Art
Buchwald, English comedians Flanders and Swann, and Bill Cosby
demonstrate typical struggles between adolescents and their parents.

007.

I. Center for Humanities.

Physical description of this set, with same sound in different forms, does not
make use of the option to give details of accompanying material in physical
description. The notes are used to explain. Added entry for publisher well known
to library patrons.

Slide set with sound accompaniment

Example of commercial cataloging by
Metro Catalog Cards

An Inquiry into the future of mankind: designing tomorrow
today. Parts I and II. (SLIDE-SOUND)
The Center for Humanities c1974
160 slides (plastic mounts) in 2 carousel cartridges. col. ; 2 x 2 in.
with phonodisc: 4s 12 in. 33⅓ rpm and 2 cassettes 1⅞ ips. 29
min.
With teacher's guide, including script and sources.

Summary: Explores man's continuing fascination with how and
why and where he is going. Because the earth's survival depends on
making intelligent judgments about the future, this interest has taken
a new, practical turn. Stresses our real ability to act in facing the
challenges of the future.

Example of pre-AACR 2 cataloging in
LC catalog *Films ...*, 1974

An Inquiry into the future of mankind: designing tomorrow today.
[Slide set] Center for Humanities, 1974.
160 slides, color, 2 x 2 in. and 2 phonodiscs (2 s. each), 12 in.,
33⅓., 29 min.
Also issued with phonotape in cassette.
With teacher's guide.
Summary: Explores man's continuing fascination with how and
why and where he is going. Stresses man's real ability to act in
facing the challenges of the future.
I. Center for Humanities.

AACR 2 cataloging

An Inquiry into the future of mankind [slide] : designing tomorrow
today. — White Plains, N.Y. : Center for Humanities, c1974.

160 slides : col. + 2 sound cassettes (29 min. : 1⅞ ips, 2 track,
mono.) + 2 sound discs (29 min. : 33⅓ rpm, mono. ; 12 in.) + 1
teacher's guide.

Slides in 2 carousel trays
Cassettes and discs with audible signal on Side 1, no signal on
Side 2.
Summary: Uses art, music, and photography to discuss need
for planning the future through use of existing and developing
technology. Suggests ways technology may affect the family,
religion, education, the arts, and the environment.
258.
I. Center for Humanities.

Study prints with sound accompaniment

> Common birds. Group I [picture]. — Chicago : Produced and
> distributed by SVE, c1963.
>
> 8 study prints : col. ; 33 x 36 cm. + 1 sound disc (28 min. :
> 33⅓ rpm, mono. ; 12 in.). — (Basic science series; PSSP - 100)
>
> Contents: Great horned own — Cardinal — Blue jay — Redwing
> blackbird — Mourning dove — Brown thrasher — Robin — Hairy
> woodpecker.
>
> Sp 104.
>
> I. Society for Visual Education.

Title proper includes indication of part. Publisher's name as appears in item, in publication statement. Series with number. Contents are unnumbered on item. Added entry for full form of publisher's name. It is known by both forms, and catalog should contain reference from SVE to full form.

**Slide set with sound accompaniment and
additional cassette**

> Musical instruments of the baroque and early classical eras [kit] /
> Division of Musical Instruments, National Museum of History
> and Technology. — Washington, D.C. : Distributed by the
> Smithsonian Institution, Office of Printing and Photographic
> Services, c1978.
>
> 58 slides : col.
> 2 sound cassettes (60 min.) : 1⅞ ips, 2 tracks, mono.
> 1 guide (22 p.) ; 20 cm.
>
> Prepared by Helen R. Hollis with assistance from James M.
> Weaver.
> Consultants: Mark Lindley, Anne Melton Kimsey.
>
> First cassette contains narration and musical examples to
> accompany slides and has audible signals for manual advance.
> Second cassette contains two baroque musical works.
>
> Summary: Shows musical instruments in the Smithsonian
> Institution and works of art which illustrate similar instruments
> played during period covered.

Statement of responsibility taken from item. Names put in notes rather than in body of entry because of length of statement and their affiliation with the responsible organization. Distribution statement from item. GMD is [kit] because package contains filmstrip with sound accompaniment and another cassette to be used separately. Physical description done according to 1.10C2., method b.

Transparency

Formation of a volcano [transparency]. — Maplewood,
   N.J. : Hammond, [19--]

1 transparency (3 overlays) : col. ; 22 x 25 cm. + 1 teacher's
manual. — (Hammond earth science transparency series)

Summary: Illustrates the active, dormant, and extinct stages in
the life of a volcano.

8558.

I. Hammond (Firm). II. Series.

VII

Description of Three-dimensional Artefacts and Realia

AACR 2 CHAPTER 10: THREE-DIMENSIONAL ARTEFACTS AND REALIA

10.0. GENERAL RULES

10.0A. SCOPE
The rules in this chapter enable the cataloger to provide a standard bibliographic description for a variety of diverse materials having in common the fact that they are three-dimensional, either naturally occurring objects or artistic or manufactured objects. The rules provided cover individual objects and multipart items which are made up of one or several three-dimensional objects. Included are artefacts, games which usually contain three-dimensional items, art works, and microscope slides or objects intended to be viewed with a microscope. Excluded from this chapter are other three-dimensional objects of a more specific nature, such as maps and globes.

10.0B. SOURCES OF INFORMATION

10.0B1. Chief source of information
Reflecting the fact that little information appears on the objects themselves, the chief source for materials of this type includes the item itself, accompanying text, and a container which is not integral to the object.

10.0B2. Prescribed sources of information
All of the information for the body of the entry can be taken from any of those parts considered to be a chief source. First examine the item itself and extract any available information. If not found there, next examine the textual accompaniment, if any, and then the container. Information for the physical description, notes, and standard number and terms of availability can be taken from any source.

10.0H. ITEMS WITH SEVERAL CHIEF SOURCES OF INFORMATION
For an item composed of two or more parts, a unifying element, often the container or textual accompaniment, is the preferable source of information for the package. Multipart packages lacking a unifying source for descriptive information relating to all of the parts are described according to 1.0H. If there is a part which functions as a first part, use it as a chief source of information. If there is no part that serves as a first part, use the part that gives the most information. Often, the part which bears the latest publication date will provide

the most information for the package. Sources of information for the description can be explained in the notes, in the order in which they relate to the description as provided for in 10.7., the notes area. Information from various parts can be combined with information for the first part or the unifying part in the description.

Teacher's manual as chief source

Booth, Ada
> The metric center [kit] / written by Ada Booth. — Rev. Sept., 1974 / reviewed and edited by Bryne Bessie Frank. — Palo Alto, Calif. : Enrich, 1974.

> Kit contains realia, models, and written teaching material.
> The title page of the teacher's guide provides information for entry.
> Collective title, dates, and statement of responsibility appear there.

In single part items with several chief sources of information, prefer a chief source bearing the latest publication date according to 1.0H2.

10.1.   TITLE AND STATEMENT OF RESPONSIBILITY AREA

10.1B.   TITLE PROPER
Record the title as instructed in 1.1B. The cataloger will often have to supply a title for items which do not have a title appearing on the item itself. In constructing a title, information can be found on a container, accompanying material, other reference sources, or publisher's catalog, according to 1.1B7. If the item is formally published, all of these sources should be checked before supplying a title. A supplied title can be a word or phrase describing all of the items contained in a grouping of objects or of a single item.

Supplied titles single items

[Conestoga wagon] [model]

[Clock face] [model]

[Robin] [realia]

[Stethoscope] [realia]

Supplied titles multipart items

[Metric measuring devices] [kit]

[Spain] [kit]

[Union soldier's costume] [realia]

10.1C.   OPTIONAL ADDITION. GENERAL MATERIAL DESIGNATION
Although the generic term used by British cataloging agencies is perhaps a better choice as a GMD for items cataloged in this chapter, North American agencies must choose from List 2 found in 1.1C1. The terms are:

diorama   model
game   realia
microscope slide

The term "realia" is used to designate any real object and is the most general of the terms from which one can choose. Any material which does not fit into the other categories would be assigned this designator.

10.1C2.
A group or multipart item containing three-dimensional materials, none of which predominates, can be assigned the GMD [kit]. Multipart items which contain a mixture of types of materials are assigned this GMD.

Use of GMD [kit]

[Spain] [kit]

(A collection of real items, models, and printed materials.)

10.1E1. Other title information
The prescribed sources for title information in this chapter include all of those defined as a chief source, including the item itself, the accompanying material, and the container. Other title information is often found on a container for objects and should be recorded here. A phrase related to the statement of responsibility that is indicative of the nature of the work is recorded as other title information according to 1.1F12.

Other title information

Battle cry [game] : American Heritage game of the Civil War. —

(The name of the company contributing to the content of the game is other title information as found on the item. Title varies. This is from the game board, not the container.)

10.1F. STATEMENTS OF RESPONSIBILITY
Statements of responsibility should be given as instructed in 1.1F., with any phrase explaining the relationship found in the chief sources. Each statement should relate to a single title proper or to the appropriate one of several titles given. Responsibility in this chapter can refer not only to creation of the content, but also to assembly for display, selection of included items, and preparation of the materials assembled.

Statement of responsibility

Dangerous parallel [game] : a simulation : decisions and consequences
in a world crisis / research and development by the Foreign
Policy Association. —

Metric survival kit [kit] / Mathematics Education Task Force,
California State Department of Education. —

Indian jewelry [realia] : a display / by Joanna Wentworth. —

Allen, Layman, E.
Wff 'n proof [game] : the game of modern logic / by Layman E.
Allen. —

10.1G. ITEMS WITHOUT A COLLECTIVE TITLE

If an item lacks a collective title and the cataloger does not supply one, individual titles can be recorded as instructed in 1.1G. If items lacking a collective title are related, a supplied collective title can be given, however. When a collective title is given, details about the pieces can be given in the physical description and in the notes.

Supplied collective title

[Metric measuring devices] [kit]

Supplied individual item titles

[Metric ruler ; litre container ; metric measuring tape ; metric grid] [kit]

10.4. PUBLICATION, DISTRIBUTION, ETC., AREA

Rules for recording information for published items in this area are found in 1.4. For items which are not actually published, that is, realia or items in their natural state which are not published, no place or name is recorded in this area according to 10.4C2. and 10.4D2.

Publication statements

Frog metamorphosis [realia]. — New York : Creative Playthings, [19--]

(Real item formally published.)

10.4F. DATE OF PUBLICATION, DISTRIBUTION, ETC.

For published materials, record the date as instructed in 1.4F. Realia which is prepared for presentation and published would be assigned a date. Realia which is not published and is an unaltered, natural object is not assigned a date according to 10.4F2. Items published with the intent that the sample would be representative of all of like items can be assigned a date of manufacture.

Date of manufacture

[Dentures] [model]. — [1978]

No date, no publication statement

[Stethoscope] [realia].

10.4G. PLACE OF MANUFACTURE, NAME OF MANUFACTURER, DATE OF MANUFACTURE

When a place and publisher are not recorded according to the above rules, the place and name of a manufacturer can be recorded as instructed in 1.4G. In recording this information, record any phrase naming the manufacturer from sources of information for this area as instructed in 1.4D3.

10.4G2.

If the manufacturer or assembler of the material is named in the statement of responsibility, it need not be repeated in this area, even though a publisher and place are missing.

10.4G3.

Optionally, the place, name and/or date of manufacture can be recorded. For some types of materials which have been manufactured by several agencies at different times, this option can add useful information and should be provided.

10.5. PHYSICAL DESCRIPTION AREA

10.5B. EXTENT OF ITEM (INCLUDING SPECIFIC MATERIAL DESIGNATION)

The number of items and a phrase chosen from those given in 10.5B1. including:

diorama	microscope slide
exhibit	mock-up
game	model

or another descriptive phrase supplied by the cataloger are recorded first in this area. Terms are not standardized in this chapter because of the diverse types of materials which it covers. Information should be concise and as specific as possible.

10.5B2.

If a group of objects cannot be described in specific designators because of the number of different types of objects involved, or because the number of some or all are difficult to determine, the physical description can be limited to a specific designator and a phrase (various pieces). Although it is not desirable because of the limited amount of information given, combined with notes under rule 10.7B10., necessary information can be recorded.

Physical description

Human vertebrae set [realia]. — Burlington, N.C. : Carolina Biological Supply, [19--]

1 vertebrae set (atlas, axis, cervical, thoracic, lumbar) : natural bone strung on nylon filament ; 42 cm. long + 1 manual.

Optional method

> 1 vertebrae set (various pieces)

> Note: Five natural bone vertebrae on nylon filament.

10.5C. OTHER PHYSICAL DETAILS
The material of which the item or items is made and the indication of color, indicating several colors, one specific color, or black and white, can be given if applicable. These can be as specific or general as the material indicates.

10.5D. DIMENSIONS
Information about the dimensions of an object and of the container can be given, when important. Dimensions of the object are important to a user, and if container size differs drastically from the size of the object, this information is also useful. However, information about the size of a container for multipart items should be given.

10.5E. ACCOMPANYING MATERIAL
Accompanying textual or sound material can be indicated according to 1.5E. Of the four methods used for recording this information, method c., recording details in a note, and method d., recording the name of the material at the end of the physical description, are preferable. The optional addition of further physical description of the material is recommended, particularly when this material requires equipment for use.

Multipart items or kits described according to the rules of this chapter often will have accompanying guides and instructions. These can be listed in the extent of the item, at the end of the physical description, or in a note.

Physical Descriptions for
Three-dimensional Artifacts and Realia

Single items

> 1 stethoscope : metal and plastic ; 58 cm. long in box, 21 x 11 x 3 cm.

> 1 pair dentures : plastic ; in box, 13 x 10 x 18 cm.

> 1 microscope slide : dry mount, col. ; 5 x 5 cm.

> 1 game (various pieces)

> Containing 12 play pieces, deck of cards and playing board.

Single item with accompanying material

> 1 human skeleton : plastic, col. ; 66 cm. long in case, 84 x 23 x 17 cm. + 1 illustrated key sheet.

Multipart items

1 game (18 capital letter cubes, 18 small letter cubes, 3 mats, 1 timer, 1 instructional manual) ; in container, 15 x 21 x 3 cm.

1 game (22 blue soldiers, 22 grey soldiers, 1 play board, die, 1 booklet) ; in container, 50 x 35 x 5 cm.

1 kit (1 grid, 1 cube, 1 ruler, 1 thermometer, 1 measuring tape, 1 spring scale, 1 mesh bag, 7 mass pieces, 1 inservice guide, 1 activities booklet) ; in container, 30 x 16 x 16 cm.

10.7. NOTE AREA

10.7B1. Nature of the item
With objects which often lack descriptive or distinctive titles, providing this note first, rather than placing all of this type of information in the summary note which appears further on in the description, can be useful. If this succinct description is sufficient, the summary can be omitted.

Notes

Adult and pupa mounted on wool. Wingless form.

Ventral ganglions with double nerve cord.

10.7B1.-5.
Notes relating to the source of the title proper are often needed when no title information is available from the prescribed sources and when titles are supplied by the cataloger. Titles on various sources often differ and recording other titles can aid in the identification of a unique item. Title information omitted from the title and statement of responsibility area because they are not needed there for identification can be given in notes.

Notes

Title supplied from supplier's catalog.

Title supplied from teacher's guide.

Title on container: American Heritage battle cry.

10.7B6. Statements of responsibility
Particularly with multipart items with collective titles, either given on the item or supplied, for which little or no information is recorded in the area for statement of responsibility, notes can supply useful information. They can relate to all parts or selected parts.

10.7B7. Edition and history
If an object or group of objects are derivatives of other creations, record the information here. It can include title and statement of responsibility and the date of the source.

Notes

Activities adapted from: The metric lab. — Sunnyvale, Calif. : Enrich, c1974.

10.7B10. Physical description

If the option in 10.5B2. is exercised to give only the specific designator and the term "various pieces" as limited description in the physical description area, notes must be given concerning the component parts. In addition, any part that requires equipment or special circumstances for use should be described in some detail. One or several notes can be given here. Even when a contents note names the various parts, a description of the characteristics of the parts is often necessary.

Notes where physical description says (various pieces)

Contains 6 interior boxes for student teams with 36 crisis manuals, 36 information file books, 36 badges, 6 Decision-choice wheels, 6 identification easels, 12 checksheet pads, 6 report pads, various group unit cards and bills.

Contains 1 teacher's box with 1 Control manual (160 p.), 1 filmstrip (62 fr.) + 1 sound disc (10 min. : 33⅓ rpm, mono. ; 7 in.), 1 Consequences calculator.

Contains 22 Union soldiers, 22 Confederate soldiers, 1 board, die + 1 booklet (30 p.)

Contains 18 red letter cubes, 18 blue letter cubes, 1 timer, and instruction book (168 p.)

10.7B11. Accompanying material

When insufficient information about accompanying material is given in the physical description area, notes are necessary. Again, this is especially true when equipment is needed for use.

Notes

Title on can: Introduction to dangerous parallel.

Instructions for play on inside of container.

Filmstrip (62 fr.) : col. ; 35 mm. + 1 sound disc (10 min. : 33⅓ rpm, mono. ; 7 in.)

Manual includes modeling directions.

10.7B14. Audience

As previously recommended, a formal note preceded by the introductory phrase "Intended audience:" is most easily located by the user of the catalog record. For some of the materials covered in this package, several types of information are useful. These can include intellectual level or grade level, specialized users, and number of people for whom an item is intended, such as the number of players for a game. This information is recorded if given in the item and is also best recorded in the manner given on the item.

> Intended audience: Grade 6 and up.

> Intended audience: Blind and physically handicapped people.

> Intended audience: Secondary students, for 36 players and teacher.

10.7B17. Summary
A summary is recommended when the combination of the title and other notes given in 10.7B1. do not clearly illustrate the nature of the contents.

> Summary: Includes specimen of worker, soldier, and winged form for low power microscopy, macrophotography, and field identification.

> Summary: Preserved frogs in 4 stages of development from tadpole to frog.

> Summary: Complete set of upper and lower teeth of an adult human demonstrating good occlusion.

> Summary: 10 whole mounts commonly used in protozoan studies.

10.7B18. Contents
Contents notes should be given when parts of a multipart item have titles, or can be specifically named.

> Contents: Ameba proteus — Cifflugia — Radiolaria — Euglena — Chilomonas — Paramecium caudatum — Stentor — Tetrahymena — Voticella — Plasmodium vivax.

> Contents: Double convex — plano convex — concavo convex — double concave — plano concave — convexo concave.

10.7B9. Numbers
Publisher's numbers relating to a single item or to a package of items should be recorded. Packages of materials gathered together from sources independent of the publisher of these packages may carry numbers for individual items. These can also be recorded.

> Kit no. 1002 ; filmstrip no. FS 1002.

> N. 502.

10.7B20. Copy being described and library's holdings
Particularly for realia, materials in their natural state, a description of the condition of the item may provide information which would affect its potential use. If these are not described in notes related to the physical description, they can be noted here.

Kit contains order form for some perishable materials.

Teacher's manual missing.

10.8D1.   Optional addition. Terms of availability

Particularly with three-dimensional objects which may require restrictions in use and circulation, these conditions of availability to the users of the collection should be noted. If an item does not circulate outside the library or if it is unavailable for interlibrary loan, this can be noted. Some of these items are commonly restricted to circulation to instructional staff for classroom use, and catalog users need to have that information.

For use in media center only.

For teacher instruction only.

For medical personnel only.

Consumable materials must be duplicated for use.

Live animal components must be ordered from company.

EXAMPLES:
Descriptive Cataloging for Three-dimensional Artefacts and Realia

Single items

Myctotherus [microscope slide]. — Skokie, Ill. : Sargent-Welch, [197-?]

1 microscope slide : col. ; 8 x 3 cm.

Summary: Cross section of large intestine of frog with this parasitic form *in situ*.

56124.

[Stethoscope] [realia]. — [19--]

1 stethoscope : metal and plastic ; 58 cm. long in box, 21 x 11 x 3 cm.

Real object described without publication information. Date is for probable date of manufacture.

A termite [microscope slide] = Isoptera. — Skokie, Ill. : Sargent-Welch, [197-?]

    1 microscope slide : dry mount, col. ; 5 x 5 cm.

    Summary: Includes specimen of worker, soldier, and winged form for low power microscopy, macrophotography, and field identification.

    57095.

      I. Title: Isoptera.

Title taken from item. Parallel title on item as well as label for parts included in summary. Other physical details appropriate for type of item.

Frog metamorphosis [realia]. — New York : Creative Playthings, [19--]

    4 frogs : imbedded in 1 plastic block, col. ; 10 x 12 x 3 cm.

    Summary: Preserved frogs in 4 stages of development from tadpole to frog.

Title from object. Physical description is supplied; specific designator with description of material in other physical details. Summary needed.

[Dentures] [model]. — [1978]

    1 pair dentures : plastic ; in box, 13 x 10 x 18 cm.

    Hinged to show action of the jaw.

    Summary: Complete set of upper and lower teeth of an adult human demonstrating good occlusion.

Supplied title. No publication information, but date of manufacture known. Use for the item described in summary.

Miniature skeleton [model]. -- Skokie, Ill. : Sargent-Welch, [197-?]

    1 human skeleton : synthetic, col. ; 66 cm. long in case, 84 x 23 x 17 cm. + 1 illustrated key sheet.

    Articulation at main joints, hands and feet molded in 1 piece, moveable mandiable.

Title from the item. Material described, length of the item and container given. Accompanying material described with terms from the item. Note relates to the nature of the item and is given first.

[Clock face with braille and raised numbers] [model]. — Louisville, Ky. (1839 Frankfort Ave., Louisville, Ky. 40206) : [Distributed by the American Printing House for the Blind, 197-?]

1 clock face : plastic, b&w ; diameter 18 cm. in container, 21 x 20 x 6 cm.

Intended audience: Blind and handicapped people.

Available free.

I. American Printing House for the Blind.

No information on item. Distribution information on label of container. Address given because of availability. Added entry for organization which is significant to users in identifying material for special audience.

Multipart items

Basic protozoology survey [microscope slide]. — [Skokie, Ill.] : Sargent-Welch, [197-?]

10 microscope slides : stained ; 8 x 3 cm.

Summary: 10 whole mounts commonly used in protozoan studies.

Contents: Ameba proteus — Difflugia — Radiolaria — Euglena — Chilomonas — Paramecium caudatum — Stentor — Tetrahymena (Conjugation) — Vorticella — Plasmodium vivax.

56164.

Title on item. Both summary and contents used, although summary could be eliminated because of information in title and contents.

Parco gene modeling kit [kit]. — Vienna, Ohio : Parco Scientific
Co., [197-?]

1 modeling kit (ca. 1000 poppit beads, 50 hydrogen bonds, 4
pairs centromeres, 3 DNA rods, 5 amino acid units) : col. + 1
teacher's guide.

In storage box.

Summary: Demonstrates DNA/RNA protein synthesis, mitosis
and meiosis, chromosome aberration, gene pool, population
genetics.

90.B-4100.

I. Title: Gene modeling kit.

Title given as on object and alternate title given added entry. Specific designator
from the item. Numbers and names of pieces given in physical description,
optionally could have been given in a note. Accompanying material relates to
whole package and is included at end of physical description. Summary shows
ways item can be used. Other title added entry.

Metric survival kit [kit] / Mathematics Education Task Force,
California State Department of Education. — Sunnyvale, Calif. :
Enrich, 1975.

1 grid, 1 cube, 1 ruler, 1 thermometer, 1 measuring tape, 1 spring
scale, 1 mesh bag, 7 mass pieces, 1 inservice guide, 1 activities
booklet ; in container, 30 x 16 x 16 cm.

Activities adapted from: The Metric lab. Sunnyvale, Calif. :
Enrich, c1974.

Intended audience: Teachers.

Summary: Manipulatives for use in teacher training with activities for use in classroom.

EN40100.

I. Mathematics Education Task Force.

Kit of objects described according to 1.10C2a. Title, statement of responsibility,
and publisher found on several parts including unifying elements, the guide, and
container. Physical description gives extent and name of each object when no
further description is necessary for each. First note relates to statement of
responsibility. Audience explained in guide. Added entry for group responsible
for content.

Physical description for above item using 10.5B2.

1 kit (1 grid, 1 cube, 1 ruler, 1 thermometer, 1 measuring tape, 1 spring scale, 1 mesh bag, 7 mass pieces) + 1 inservice guide + 1 activities booklet ; in container, 30 x 16 x 16 cm.

Physical description using 10.5B2. option or 1.10C3c. and note relating to physical description

16 various pieces.

Contains 1 grid, 1 cube, 1 ruler, 1 thermometer, 1 measuring tape, 1 spring scale, 1 mesh bag, 7 mass pieces, 1 inservice guide, 1 activities booklet.

In container 30 x 16 x 16 cm.

Booth, Ada.
   The metric center [kit] / written by Ada Booth. — Rev. Sept., 1974 / reviewed and edited by Bryne Bessie Frank. — Palo Alto, Calif. : Enrich, 1974.

1 tape measure, 1 thermometer, 2 rulers, 1 container of stacking masses, 1 cube, 10 rods, 20 activity masters, 6 performance tests, 10 cartridges, 1 Telor device, 1 teacher's manual ; in container, 35 x 21 x 13 cm.

Interchangeable programmed learning cartridges to be used with Telor device.

Intended audience: Grade 6 and up.

Summary: Laboratory oriented approach to the metric system and measurement.

No. S02.

Main entry for author of activities. Materials gathered and manufactured to use with activities. Edition statement in teacher's guide, unifying element. Some parts have c1973, but item published in 1974. First note relates to physical description.

Organisms [kit]. — [2nd ed.]. — [Boston] : American Science and Engineering, c1978.

1 kit (various pieces) : col. ; in box, 60 x 80 x 40 cm. — (SCIS II. Life science)

Original Science curriculum improvement study (SCIS) series developed at Lawrence Hall of Science, University of California, Berkeley.

Senior author: Lester Paldy.

Second ed. includes new Teacher guides, content, activity cards, duplicating master booklets to replace student manuals.

Contents: Drawer 1 (1 teacher's guide, 1 set SDM's, 1 set activity cards, 2 order forms, 38 planter cups, 36 planter bases, 4 packs seeds, 3 sprinklers, 16 trays, 1 wax marker) — Drawer 2 (5 containers) — Drawer 3 (4 containers, 1 light source) — Drawer 4 (2 nets, 32 magnifiers, fish food, 5 medicine droppers, 32 tumblers, 10 lids, 1 thermometer) — Drawer 5 (1 baster, 6 funnels, 20 filter discs) — Drawer 6 (16 vials, 16 caps) — Sand and soil box.

Order forms included for live animals and vegetation, including guppies, snails, anacharis, duckweed, algae, foxtail, foninallis, and daphnia culture.

Audience: Elementary school.

Summary: A 16-week materials-centered course of study containing 12 units covering concepts including organism, birth, death, habitat, food web, detritus, and growth.

8339-1100.

I. Science Curriculum Improvement Study. II. Series: SCIS II. III. Series: Life science.

Edition statement found in guide. Note on edition and explanation of SCIS necessary for added entry. Contents explained in note relating to physical description. One note for materials which must be ordered. Audience and summary from guide. Added entries for series and subseries.

Battle cry [game] : American Heritage game of the Civil War. — Springfield, Mass. : Milton Bradley, c1962.

1 game (22 blue soldiers, 22 grey soldiers, 1 board, die) + 1 booklet ; in container, 50 x 35 x 5 cm.

Instructions on inside of box lid.

Booklet entitled: The Civil War : an outline history / prepared by the editors of American Heritage.

Intended audience: Ages 9 to adult.

Summary: Game for 2 or 4 players allows students to simulate battles described in booklet and recreate the Civil War.

I. American Heritage Publishing Co.

Title from game board as chief source. Title differs on container. For games, summary can indicate number of players.

—————

Dangerous parallel [game] : a simulation : decisions and consequences in a world crisis / research and development by the Foreign Policy Association. — Glenview, Ill. : Scott Foresman, c1969.

1 game (various pieces) ; in container, 33 x 50 x 26 cm.

Contains 6 interior boxes for student teams with 36 crisis manuals, 36 information file books, 36 badges, 6 decision-choice wheels, 6 identification easels, 12 checksheet pads, 6 report pads, various troop unit cards and bills.

Contains 1 teacher's box with 1 Control manual (160 p.) + 1 filmstrip (62 fr.) + 1 sound disc (10 min. : $33\frac{1}{3}$ rpm, mono. ; 7 in.) + 1 Consequences calculator.

Summary: Six teams of 3 or 4 players from fictionalized nations participate in negotiations and decision-making.

3967.

I. Foreign Policy Association.

Title contains two parts in other title information. Statement of responsibility appears prominently in guide, unifying element. Physical description abbreviated because of large number of diverse parts. Note on physical description divided into two parts for clarity. No intended audience prominent on item. Information put into summary.

—————

Allen, Layman E.
Wff 'n proof [game] : the game of modern logic / by Layman E. Allen. — 1972 ed. — New Haven, Conn. : Autotelic Instructional Materials ; Turtle Creek, Pa. : Wuff 'n Proof [distributor], 1972, c1962.

1 game (18 capital letter cubes, 18 small letter cubes, 3 mats, 1 timer) + 1 instruction manual (168 p.) ; in container, 15 x 21 x 3 cm.

Intended audience: Age 6 through adult.

Summary: Twenty-one games for 2 to 4 players involving logic and abstract thinking.

I. Title.

Entry and statement of responsibility prominent on item. Edition statement as it appears on item. Places different for publisher and distributor. Designation added for distributor. Audience on item.

Allen, Robert W.
The propaganda game [game] / by Robert W. Allen, Lorne Greene. — 1972 ed. — New Haven, Conn. : Autotelic Instructional Materials, 1972, c1966.

1 game (40 example cards, 4 technique cards, 4 tokens, 1 clear thinking chart) + 1 instruction manual ; in container, 15 x 13 x 3 cm.

Based on: Thinking straighter / by George Henry Moulds.

Intended audience: For teenagers and adults.

Summary: Designed for 2 to 4 players to introduce techniques used to distort thinking.

I. Greene, Lorne. II. Title.

VIII
Description of Microforms

11.0. GENERAL RULES

Rules in this chapter cover all types of publications in micro formats, those which are either opaque or transparent and are not easily visible to the naked eye. The reason for treating these materials as nonprint, although much of the material on microforms is print, is that equipment is needed in order to read or view the contents. Because much of what appears in microforms is previously published material, often monographs or serials, and occasionally, graphics and maps in reduced form, the provisions of these rules have not met with universal acceptance. A recent statement in *Cataloging Service Bulletin*, no. 11 (Winter, 1981) outlines an interim decision by several of our major libraries:

> Because of the imminence of the adoption of the *Anglo-American Cataloguing Rules*, second edition, the Library of Congress, the National Agricultural Library, and the National Library of Medicine have had to make an interim decision about the cataloging of microforms that reproduce previously published books and serials. Such microform materials are currently being discussed in a debate between those who believe that the original publication should be emphasized with data relating to the microform placed in a secondary position (essentially the AACR principle) and those who believe that the microform should be emphasized instead (essentially the AACR 2 principle). At the request of the Association of Research Libraries and other library groups and pending a resolution of the problems the Library of Congress, the National Agricultural Library, and the National Library of Medicine will continue to follow the AACR 1 principle for bibliographic description when cataloging microforms for previously published books and serials. For choice and form of access points, however, the libraries named will apply AACR 2. Details regarding this implementation will be disseminated through the normal cataloging channels.

The final Library of Congress policy for the cataloging of microreproductions appears in LC's *Cataloging Service Bulletin*, no. 14, Fall, 1981, pp. 56-58. The policy applies to microreproductions including books, pamphlets, and printed sheets; cartographic materials; manuscripts; music; serials; and to macroreproductions, particularly of graphic materials which are produced "on demand." Catalogers should refer to this explanation of the "rule interpretation" which gives details about bibliographic description. Most libraries will want to follow the direction of the major institutions. Discussion and examples of microforms cataloged according to *AACR 2* rules in this part of the text will, therefore, be limited to items originally published in microformats.

11.0A. SCOPE
Rules are included for microforms on film (in reels, cassettes, and cartridges), on fiche, on microopaque cards, and secured in aperture cards of which the microform is only a part.

11.0B. SOURCES OF INFORMATION
The chief source differs from one form to another. For film, the source is the title frame(s) which usually appear at the beginning of the film; however, more than one frame can be considered as the chief source. The chief source for fiche and opaques is also the title frame(s), but in the absence of sufficient information there, it can be taken without brakets from the eye-readable printed material on the item. The chief source for an aperture card is the first card of a set or the card itself of a single item. Other sources in order of preference are:

- the rest of the item, including first the microform itself and then an integral container such as a cassette, etc.

- a separate container

- accompanying material

- any other source.

Examine the chief source and extract information for:

Area 1. Title and statement of responsibility
  2. Edition
  3. Special data for cartographic material and serials
  4. Publication, distribution, etc.
  6. Series

If the information is not found in the chief source, examine the rest of the item itself and an integral container, plus a separate container for the following areas:

Area 2. Edition
  3. Special data for cartographic material and serials
  4. Publication, distribution, etc.
  6. Series

Information for the following areas can be taken from any source:

Area 5. Physical description
  7. Notes
  8. Standard number and terms of availability

11.1. TITLE AND STATEMENT OF RESPONSIBILITY AREA

11.1B. TITLE PROPER
Title proper is recorded according to general instructions in 1.1B.

11.1C. OPTIONAL ADDITION. GENERAL MATERIAL DESIGNATION
If only original microform publications are cataloged according to these rules, this GMD will not contradict the form of the content of the material and should be used.

Parallel titles, other title information, and statements of responsibility are recorded as instructed in 1.1. Original microform publications often have several names related to the statement of responsibility. In order to be recorded in the body of the entry, they should appear prominently in the chief source of information. Rules 1.1F5. and 1.1F6. should aid the cataloger in choosing and recording these names.

11.1G. ITEMS WITHOUT A COLLECTIVE TITLE
As with other types of materials, several items may be published on one or several physical items published together without a collective title. They can be described as a unit or as separate items. Although either method is adequate, providing separate entries may be preferable because the entries for separate parts are more easily understood by the user and more detailed information about the physical description and location of each of the parts can be given. Also, the title elements are given separately which avoids the confusion of recording several titles and statements of responsibility in one area. When cataloged separately, a "with note" as shown in 11.7B21. is used.

11.2. EDITION AREA
Edition statements are recorded as instructed in 1.2B. LC will not apply the optional rule in 11.2B3. which allows for the inclusion of edition information, not appearing on the item, in the body of the description.

11.3. SPECIAL DATA FOR CARTOGRAPHIC MATERIALS AND SERIALS
As mentioned above, LC and other major libraries are intending to catalog serials in microformats according to the rules for the original publication. It is likely that this change from *AACR 2* will also be applied to republication of cartographic materials in microforms. If the microform is cartographic material, see the instructions in 3.3. for rules, and the discussion about this area in this text.

11.4. PUBLICATION, DISTRIBUTION, ETC., AREA
Determining the information for this area for original microform publications should not pose any difficult problems if the rules in 1.1. are followed. The place, name, and date should be associated with the facts of the publication in the microformat. LC will apply 11.4E. which allows for the optional addition of a statement of function of publisher, distributor, in this area, on a case by case basis. The date given should be the date on which the microform was published.

11.5. PHYSICAL DESCRIPTION AREA

Aperture cards are data cards which may or may not contain eye-readable information on the card. They are usually key punched for automated retrieval. If cataloged according to *AACR 2*, the information on the microfiche insert in the card is used for description. Microfiche are sheets of base material containing frames of microimages. Microfilm is contained on reels, in cartridges, or cassettes and is composed of frames of microimages running parallel to either the width or length of the film. All of these formats are filmed on a transparent base, and the images themselves can be either positive or negative. A positive image appears to be the same as an eye-readable copy, dark letters on a light opaque background, while a negative microform reverses this, with light letters on a dark background. If hard copy is made from a microform, the copy is usually produced in the opposite image (positive or negative) from the microimages on the film or fiche. Hence, a positive microform produces negative hard copy, and a negative microform produces positive copy. Microopaques contain microimages on an opaque background.

11.5B1. Extent of item (including specific material designation)

In describing the extent of the item in 11.5B1., LC has decided not to drop the prefix "micro" from the specific designator. Most libraries will want to retain the prefix to avoid unnecessary confusion for the user. The type of microform given in either the singular or plural is offered in the extent statement. The number of frames for microfiche is easily calculated and should be given; however, although the number of frames on film differs greatly, this information is difficult to determine and can be inferred from other description.

11.5C. OTHER PHYSICAL DETAILS

Although negative film is as common as positive, rule 11.5C1. instructs the cataloger to record the information only when the images are negative. According to 11.5C2. and C3., information about illustrations and color should be given. Specific directions for recording dimensions of the different forms are given in 11.5D. Accompanying material is described according to 1.5E. and will be included on a case by case basis by LC.

11.6. SERIES AREA

Series relating to the microform are to be recorded as instructed in 1.6.

11.7. NOTE AREA

If described according to the rules for the original publication, the directions given in 11.7B. will not apply to materials cataloged in this chapter, because they will not be reproductions of other formats. All of the notes will relate to the microform.

11.7B1. Nature, scope, or artistic or other form of an item

This note may be useful for collections of materials lacking a collective title which are cataloged as a unit.

11.7B3. Source of title proper
The location of the title proper should be noted if it is not taken from the chief source of information.

11.7B6. Statements of responsibility
Where several names or bodies are associated with the publication, and some are omitted from the statement of responsibility because they are not given prominently in the chief source or are not deemed important for the agency, notes should be given with names and designation of the nature of the responsibility. This is particularly helpful when several groups have sponsored or endorsed a particular publication and are not mentioned in the body of the entry.

11.7B9. Publication, distribution, etc.
If not clear from the body of the description, the function of those named in the body can be clarified here. Also, additional information, not mentioned in the body, can be given here.

11.7B10. Physical description
The reduction ratio can vary on all types of microforms. This information is important because the material should be viewed with a reader which is equipped with a lens appropriate for the reduction ratio of the film. Two common reduction ratios are 19 x and 21 x; a common range is between 16 x and 30 x. If the ratio falls outside that range, notes should be made according to the directions with one of the phrases suggested. Because in the higher reduction ranges a more exact match between the characteristics of the equipment and the film is necessary, the ratio should be given for materials in the ultra-high reduction range.

11.7B13. Dissertations
Many dissertations are originally published in microforms, and this note should be given as instructed in 2.7B13.

11.7B16. Other formats available
If hard copy of a microform is available, this information can be noted here.

11.7B17. Summary
A summary may eliminate the need for a scope or contents note and can be used for this purpose.

11.7B18. Contents
Either a formal contents note or a phrase describing all or parts of the contents is suggested in this rule. However, if the information covers the nature, scope, or form of an item, it should be given under 11.7B1. If parts are titled, a contents note may be preferable to a summary, although both can be used.

11.7B19. Numbers
Many microforms are assigned numbers by their publishers and should be noted here, unless they are international standard numbers which are given in 11.8B.

11.7B20. Copy being described and library's holdings
Information on the title frames will often indicate peculiarities of the copy which should be noted for the user.

11.7B21. "With" notes
These notes should be given for items lacking a collective title which are cataloged separately, as is suggested.

11.8D. Optional addition. Terms of availability
LC has determined that this information will be given for microforms. However, it may not be essential for other libraries.

EXAMPLES:
Descriptive Cataloging for Original Microforms

Rawnsley, David E.
    A comparison of guides to non-print media [microform] / David E. Rawnsley. — Stanford, Calif. : ERIC Clearinghouse on Educational Media and Technology, 1973.

    1 microfiche (41 fr.) : negative ; 11 x 15 cm.

    Summary: Bibliographic and contents information about 66 indexes and guides to non-print instructional media.

    ED 083 837.

        I. Title.

Entry under author prominently named. The clearinghouse is located at the university, but the place is listed in publication area, not the institution in which the publisher is located. Negative print is noted. Number from publisher is noted. No standard number assigned.

Dodge, Bernard J.
Audiovisual resources for teaching instructional technology
[microform] : an annotated listing / Bernard J. Dodge. — Syracuse,
N.Y. : ERIC Clearinghouse on Information Resources, 1978.

1 microfiche (77 fr.) : negative ; 11 x 15 cm.

For teachers of instructional technology.

Summary: A compilation of audiovisual resources for teaching
about educational technology.

ED 152 337.

Available from Syracuse University Printing Services, 125 College
Place, Syracuse, N.Y. 13210. (IR-23, $4.00 plus postage for hard
copy).

I. Title.

Intended audience on the item. Availability of hard copy noted. If hard copy had
been available in the library, a separate entry would be preferable, although it
could be included in notes.

———————

Coulson, John E.
Systems analysis in education [microform] / John E. Coulson
and John F. Cogswell ; Systems Development Corporation. —
Springfield, Va. : Clearinghouse for Federal Scientific and Technical Information, 1965.

1 microfiche (19 fr.) : negative ; 11 x 15 cm.

Presented at the Conference on Development and Use of Data
Banks for Educational Research, Boston, Dec. 4, 1964.

AD 611865.

SDC professional report SP 1863.

Available from the publisher: Microfiche, $.50, hard copy
$1.00.

I. Cogswell, John. II. Title.

Entry under personal author first named. Statements of responsibility includes
corporate author prominently named. Conference given in note which provides
information for tracing, if desired. Publisher's number and corporate report
number both given.

———————

Bazelak, Leonard Paul.
A content analysis of tenth-grade students' responses to Black literature [microform] : including the effects of reading this literature on attitudes toward race / Leonard Paul Bazelak. — Ann Arbor, Mich. : University Microfilms, 1973.

1 microfilm reel ; 35 mm.

Theses (Ed.D.) — Syracuse University, 1973.

74-8334.

I. Title.

Madison, John Paul.
An analysis of values and social action in multi-racial children's literature [microform] / John Paul Madison. — Ann Arbor, Mich. : University Microfilms, 1973.

1 microfilm reel ; 35 mm.

Thesis (Ed.D.) — University of Illinois at Urbana-Champaign, 1972.

73-17308.

I. Title.

Two dissertations with note indicating this.

IX
Access Points for Nonprint

AACR 2 CHAPTER 21: CHOICE OF ACCESS POINTS

21.0. INTRODUCTORY RULES

After the cataloger has determined the content of the bibliographic description for a nonprint item, access points or headings are chosen to enable the user to locate the bibliographic record under main and added entries which relate to the persons, corporate bodies, and titles associated with the item.

21.0B. SOURCES FOR DETERMINING ACCESS POINTS

The preferred sources of information for choice of access points are closely related to the chief source(s) of information discussed in 1.0A., 1.1A2., and in the rules for sources of information for each of the formats. Particularly, the source(s) of information for determining the content of the title and the statement of responsibility area for each of the formats are used. These rules are found in each chapter under the mnemonic numbering structure .0B. "Sources of Information," following the various chapter numbers. As we have seen, the chief source and acceptable substitutes differ from chapter to chapter and are not the same for different types of formats. This rule strongly suggests that only statements appearing prominently in the chief source, substitutes for the chief source, or in the content of the item be considered. Information found in sources outside the item are to be considered only when statements appearing in the chief source are "ambiguous or insufficient."

These general directions may eliminate access points which are necessary for users of nonprint materials. Some of the information provided in the title and statement of responsibility area and in notes related to title and responsibility information may be important access points for users of the material. Also, some information placed in the publication, distribution, etc., area and even in notes related to this area may prove useful as access points for nonprint. Certainly, the relationship of a chosen access point should be made clear in the bibliographic description, but to limit the choice of those points in the way suggested may not give adequate access to the users of the nonprint catalog.

Information provided in these areas, 1 and 4, can be limited or expanded according to options found in related rules. The amount of information given in the body of the description and in the notes can vary according to the cataloger's understanding of the importance of the persons and groups named in relation to the publication of the item and in relation to the needs of the users of a particular collection. Just as the knowledge of the cataloger comes into play when determining the information to be presented in the description, it is also a key factor in deciding the provision of access points based on that description. Many libraries concerned with comprehensive access may want to modify the strict application of this general rule, 21.0B. Access points based on information not found in the chief source and not even given in the body of the entry, but found in the notes may be necessary for the item and beneficial for the user.

21.1. BASIC RULE

21.1A. WORKS OF PERSONAL AUTHORSHIP

21.1A1. Definition

A person who is chiefly responsible for intellectual and/or artistic content of a nonprint item is considered to be a "personal author." Such individuals can include artists, photographers, cartographers, composers, and in some cases, producers, directors, animators, or other individuals responsible for an original concept and general production of nonprint materials. In some cases, performers whose performance constitutes the content of a sound or a sound and visual presentation are considered to be personally responsible for the item and therefore, are considered "personal authors" of the presentation. Their relationship to the item, however, must go beyond the performance of material conceived by another individual or group.

21.1A2. General rule

If one or more individuals are responsible for the intellectual content or artistic content of a nonprint item, entry should be under the heading for that person responsible, the person principally responsible if more than one person is named, or the first person named in cases of "mixed personal authorship." If more than one personal author is named, entry is under the first one named.

21.1B. ENTRY UNDER A CORPORATE BODY

21.1B1. Definition

Corporate bodies which are most often responsible for the content of a nonprint item are associations, institutions, particularly educational institutions, nonprofit enterprises, government agencies, and conferences.

21.1B2. General rule

The general rule for entry under a corporate body is restricted to certain types of content emanating from a corporate body, for nonprint material this seldom applies. They include materials:

a. of an administrative nature related to the body itself

b. legal and governmental utterances

c. the collective thought of the body

d. the collective activity of the body

e. the collective activity of a group going beyond mere performance.

The collective thought of a corporate body, such as a sound tape or videotape of a corporate report or taped or filmed meetings or deliberations which are collective activities of a corporate body, would qualify under c. and d. above. A sound or visual production of a performing individual or group performing their own material originating in the performance would qualify under e. above.

These rules for corporate entry are much more restrictive than previously used rules. Relatively few nonprint items will fall into one of the five categories. Few groups named in a statement of responsibility will be chosen as main entry. Corporate publishers, whether commercial or nonprofit, will also not be used as a main entry, in most cases. In case of doubt about the nature of content emanating from a corporate body, do not enter the item under a corporate main entry.

21.1C.   ENTRY UNDER TITLE

Title entry is used under several sets of circumstances which are common to nonprint materials.

1.   when personal responsibility is unknown or diffuse.

Diffuse responsibility is defined in 21.6C2. as responsibility "shared between more than three persons or corporate bodies and principal responsibility is not attributed to any one, two, or three." This rule also suggests that an added entry be made under the first named person or group responsible. As mentioned above, added entries may be necessary for nonprint items for more than the first named.

2.   when the work does not emanate from a corporate body.

With a nonprint item which has several persons or groups named relating to intellectual or artistic content on the item, the cataloger may choose to use none, one, or several in the statement of responsibility area. Information omitted from the statement of responsibility can be given in notes. Even when one or two names are given in the statement of responsibility, this rule of diffuse authorship would apply and entry is likely to be under title, as the rule indicates.

3.   when an item is a collection or edited work.

Edited works are uncommon for nonprint. Collections are more common, but are usually sound recordings which are covered in more specific rules for that type of format found in 21.23., Entry of Sound Recordings. Entry for those collections which are not sound recordings are covered in 21.7. They include collections of independent works by different persons or groups, complete or extracted works, contributions to a collected work produced under editorial direction, or a mixture of any of the above. Entry under title would be made for items with a collective title according to rule 21.7B. Lacking a collective title, entry would be made under the heading for the first item in the collection which could be under title, person, or group responsible for the first item.

21.4.   WORKS FOR WHICH A SINGLE PERSON OR CORPORATE BODY IS RESPONSIBLE

Works for which one person or group is responsible are entered under the heading appropriate for that person or group.

21.8. WORKS OF MIXED RESPONSIBILITY. MODIFICATIONS OF OTHER WORKS

Although nonprint items would seem to fall into this category, the scope note in 21.8A. reveals that the mixed contributions covered in these rules are not those commonly associated with nonprint. Modifications of existing works, such as a film version of a novel, would be entered under the heading appropriate for the film according to 21.9. Any modification which is different from the original medium of expression, any nonprint version or treatment of a print item, would be entered under its own heading.

21.16. ADAPTATIONS OF ART WORKS

Materials which could be described by using Chapter 8 or Chapter 10 might fall into the category covered by this rule. An adaptation from one graphic medium to another would be entered under the heading for the adaptor. A reproduction of a graphic, however, would be entered under the heading for the original work. Collections of reproductions of one artist are entered under the heading for the artist according to rule 21.17. Reproductions with text, if the person writing the text is named prominently in the chief source of information, would be entered under the author.

21.23. ENTRY OF SOUND RECORDINGS

21.23A.

A sound recording of one work, either music or spoken word, is entered under the heading for the work. Added entries are made for performers when they are named prominently.

21.23B.

A sound recording which is a collection of works by the same person is entered under the heading for those works, usually the personal author or person responsible. Added entries can be made for the principal performers. The rule indicates that if there are more than three performers, an added entry should be made only for the first named. Some libraries may want to make added entries for all performers or more than three if they are important access points for users.

21.23C.

Enter a sound recording of works by different persons, performed by the same person or several persons under the heading for the principal performer. If two or more persons are named as performers, enter the recording under the heading for the first named performer and make added entries under the headings for other performers or performing groups. This rule is intended for those productions where the performers are the unifying element.

21.23D.

If a sound recording contains works by different persons and is performed by more than three principal performers or by several performers, none of whom is indicated to be a principal performer, enter it under the collective title. Items without a collective title would be entered under the heading for the first work according to 21.7C. If the cataloger chooses to separately describe each item in the collection without a collective title, the entry for each part would be the heading appropriate for that part (see 6.1G.).

21.29. GENERAL RULE FOR ADDED ENTRIES

Access points provided by added entries are extremely important for nonprint materials. The main entry heading for nonprint will often be a title. Access to items with a title main entry should be provided by making added entries, which would be of use to the library patron, for all of the persons and groups associated with the responsibility for the item. It should be remembered that some of the rules for main entry instruct the cataloger to make added entries for specific types of individuals or groups. These rules are not restrictive, however. They include suggestions for names which should always be given an added entry. They do not restrict the use of additional added entries which can provide necessary access to the user.

Any heading, either a title or person or corporate name, under which the user may assume a nonprint item could be found is a candidate for an added entry. Rule 21.29D. instructs the cataloger to make added entries which seem appropriate "in the context of a given catalogue." In addition, added entries need not necessarily be based only on the information given in the body of the entry. For example, notes related to title and statement of responsibility and to publication might provide information which would be the basis for an added entry heading. This is important for cataloging agencies which choose to eliminate information from these areas in the body which can be given in notes.

21.30. SPECIFIC RULES FOR ADDED ENTRIES

These rules describe specific types of instances or relationships of individual, corporate, or other names which should suggest an added entry. Generally, when one, two, or three names are associated in a given capacity with the item, added entries are made for all three names. If four or more persons or bodies are similarly associated, an added entry is made under the heading for the first named. However, if the agency finds it important to go beyond the specific rules in 21.30., rule 21.29D. gives license to do so. Those categories for consideration for added entries which are particularly important for nonprint include collaborators, writers, corporate bodies, and related works.

21.30B. COLLABORATORS

With a person or corporate author entry, make added entries for up to two additional collaborators. If the entry is under title, make added entries for up to three collaborating persons, or if more than three are named, make added entries for the first named. Again, this rule can be set aside if the cataloger finds more names necessary for the item and the user.

21.30C. WRITERS

If entry is under title, other person, or corporate body, make an added entry for any prominently named person responsible for content.

21.30E. CORPORATE BODIES

Any prominently named corporate body, whether it be a profit or nonprofit organization, can be given an added entry. However, excluded from this provision are distributors and manufacturers. Included are publishers which may perform functions beyond the business function of publication. Many publishers of nonprint materials do contribute beyond the business function of publishing and in some cases they will be named in the statement of responsibility. In some instances, the cataloger may choose to name them only in the publication, distribution area. If their function is sufficiently broad, an added entry can be made under the heading for the body, whether it appears in the body of the entry in either area or in the notes. Many publishers of nonprint materials are thought of as authors by catalog users. Under this rule and under 21.29B., catalogers will want to consider making added entries for publishers of nonprint.

21.30G. RELATED WORKS

Nonprint items based on other nonprint and print materials, or associated with other published items in any way, may need to be related to those items in the catalog with the use of notes and access points based on those notes. Remakes, sequels, reissues with different titles, or other authors and titles related to the item being cataloged may provide valuable access to nonprint media.

Appendix I
Cataloging Aids

CATALOGING RULES

Anglo-American Cataloguing Rules. Second Edition. Edited by M. Gorman and P. W. Winkler. Chicago: American Library Association, 1978.

Anglo-American Cataloging Rules: North American Text. Chicago: American Library Association, 1967.

REVISIONS OF AACR 1

Anglo-American Cataloging Rules: North American Text: Chapter 6 Separately Published Monographs. Chicago: American Library Association, 1974.

Anglo-American Cataloging Rules: North American Text: Chapter 12 Revised: Audio-visual and Special Instructional Materials. Chicago: American Library Association, 1975.

Anglo-American Cataloging Rules: North American Text: Chapter 14 Revised: Sound Recordings. Chicago: American Library Association, 1976.

INTERNATIONAL STANDARD BIBLIOGRAPHIC DESCRIPTIONS

ISBD(CM): International Standard Bibliographic Description for Cartographic Materials. London: International Federation of Library Associations, Office for Universal Bibliographic Control, 1977.

ISBD(G): General International Standard Bibliographic Description: Annotated Text. London: International Federation of Library Associations, International Office for Universal Bibliographic Control, 1977.

ISBD(M): International Standard Bibliographic Description for Monographic Publications. rev. ed. London: International Federation of Library Associations, International Office for Universal Bibliographic Control, 1978.

ISBD(NBM): International Standard Bibliographic Description for Non-Book Materials. London: International Federation of Library Associations, International Office for Universal Bibliographic Control, 1977.

ISBD(M): International Standard Bibliographic Description for Printed Music. London: International Federation of Library Associations, International Office for Universal Bibliographic Control, 1979.

LIBRARY OF CONGRESS CATALOGS IN BOOK FORM

(Selected titles containing nonprint materials. For distribution see any recent LC catalog.)

National Union Catalog
    1953-57. 1958. 28v. Reprint.
    1958-62. Out of print. Film and music parts still in print, as listed below.
    1956-67. 125v.
    1963-67. Out of print. Film and music parts still in print, as listed below.
    1968-72. 1973. 128v.
    1973. 16v.
    1974. 18v.
    1975. 17v.
    1976. 16v.

FILM CATALOGS

Library of Congress Catalog—Motion Pictures and Filmstrips. (Included in *National Union Catalog* through 1976, available separately as cited.)

    Films and Other Materials for Projection
    1973, 1974.
    1975.
    1976.
    1977. Two semi-annual issues.
    1973-77. 7v. In book form and microform.
    1978.

    Audiovisual Materials
    1979.
    1980. Three quarterly issues and annual cumulation.

MICROFORM CATALOGS

National Register of Microform Masters. (Included in *National Union Catalog* through 1973, available separately as cited.)
    1969.
    1970.
    1971.
    1972.
    1973.
    1974.
    1965-75. 6v.
    1976.
    1977.
    1978.
    1979.

MUSIC CATALOGS

Library of Congress Catalog — Music and Phonorecords. (Included in *National Union Catalog* through 1976, available separately as cited.)

Music, Books on Music, and Sound Recordings.
1973.
1974.
1975.
1976.
1973-77. 8v. In book form and microform.
1978.
1979.
1980. Current subscription. One semi-annual and annual cumulation.

CATALOGING INFORMATION FROM LIBRARY OF CONGRESS

Library of Congress Information Bulletin. (ISSN 0041-7904). (Available from LC Central Services Division, Printing and Processing Section, Washington, DC 20540.)

See particularly:

"AACR 2 Options Proposed by the Library of Congress, Chapters 2-11." *Library of Congress Information Bulletin* 38 (August 10, 1979): 307-308.

"AACR 2 Options to Be Followed by the Library of Congress, Chapters 1-2, 21, 26." *Library of Congress Information Bulletin* 37 (July 21, 1978): 422-28.

Library of Congress Cataloging Service Bulletin. (ISSN 0160-8029). (Available from LC Cataloging Distribution Service, Washington, DC 20541.)

See particularly each issue since 11 and

"Descriptive Cataloging, AACR 2, Library of Congress Rule Interpretations." *Cataloging Service Bulletin* 11 (Winter 1981): 3-53.

"Descriptive Cataloging, AACR 2, Part I. Introduction and Rule Interpretation." *Cataloging Service Bulletin* 10 (Fall 1980): 4-14.

"Descriptive Cataloging, AACR 2, General Material Designations (GMD's) and Uniform Titles, Copyright Dates." *Cataloging Service Bulletin* 10 (Fall 1980): 14-15.

"Descriptive Cataloging, AACR 2, Options to Be Followed by the Library of Congress, Paragraphing ..., Spacing ..., Tracings...." *Cataloging Service Bulletin* 8 (Spring 1980): 8-15.

"AACR 2: Cartographic Materials." *Cataloging Service Bulletin* 7 (Winter 1980): 3.

"Descriptive Cataloging, AACR 2, Errata ..., Display of General Material Designations, Implementation ..., Rule Interpretations for AACR 2." *Cataloging Service Bulletin* 6 (Fall 1979): 2-26.

"Descriptive Cataloging, AACR 2." *Cataloging Service Bulletin* 5 (Summer 1979): 3-9.

MARC FORMATS

Library of Congress. *Maps: A MARC Format.* Second Edition. Washington, DC: Superintendent of Documents, 1976.

Library of Congress. *Music: A MARC Format.* Washington, DC: Superintendent of Documents, 1976.

Library of Congress. *Films: A MARC Format.* Washington, DC: Superintendent of Documents, 1970.

National Level Bibliographic Record—Films. Washington, DC: Library of Congress, Cataloging Distribution Service, 1981.

National Level Bibliographic Record—Music. Washington, DC: Library of Congress, Cataloging Distribution Service. To be issued Fall 1981.

OCLC FORMATS

Audiovisual Media Format. Columbus, OH: OCLC, Inc., 1980 (revised June 1981).

Bibliographic Input Standards. Columbus, OH: OCLC, Inc., 1980.

Sound Recording Format. Columbus, OH: OCLC, Inc., 1980.

Appendix II
Background Reading: AACR 2 and
Bibliographic Control of Nonprint

"AACR 2 Background and Summary." *Library of Congress Information Bulletin* 47 (October 20, 1978): 640-52.

Anderson, Dorothy. *Universal Bibliographic Control: A Long Term Policy — A Plan for Action*. Munich: Verlag Dokumentation, Pullach, 1974.

"Anglo-American Cataloguing Committee for Cartographic Material Formed." *Library of Congress Information Bulletin* 38 (November 2, 1979): 456-57.

Brown, James W., ed. *Nonprint Media Information Networking: Status and Potentials*. Washington, DC: ERIC Clearinghouse on Information Resources, 1979. (ED 126 857).

Chibnall, Bernard. *The Organization of Media*. Hamden, CT: Linnett Books, 1976.

Chisholm, Margaret. "Problems and Directions in Bibliographic Organization of Media." In *Reader in Media Technology and Libraries*, edited by Margaret Chisholm. Englewood, CO: Microcard Editions, 1975.

"Code Revision — A New International Standard." *Library Resources and Technical Services* (Winter 1976): 91-93.

Croghan, Anthony. *A Bibliographic System for Non-book Media: A Description and List of Works*. London: Coburg Publications, 1976.

Davidson, D. E. "Bibliographic Control of Audiovisual Materials." *Catalogue & Index* 50 (1978): 3-4.

Fleischer, Eugene, and Helen Goodman. *Cataloging Audiovisual Materials*. New York: Neal-Schuman, 1980. [A problem/workbook for AACR 2 cataloging.]

Gardhouse, Judy. "NFB (National Film Board of Canada) Develops Delivery Service for Canadian Nonprint Media." *Canadian Library Journal* (April 1980): 73-76.

Gorman, Michael. "The Anglo-American Cataloguing Rules, Second Edition." *Library Resources & Technical Services* 22 (Summer 1978): 209-226.

Gorman, Michael. *The Concise AACR 2: Being a Rewritten and Simplified Version of Anglo-American Cataloguing Rules*, Second Edition. Chicago: American Library Association, 1981.

Hagler, Ronald. *Where's That Rule? A Cross-Index of the Two Editions of the Anglo-American Cataloguing Rules*. Ottawa, ON: Canadian Library Association, 1979.

Hinton, Frances. "The Concise AACR 2." *Library Resources and Technical Services* (April/June 1981): 204-206.

Hoffmann, Christa F. B. *Getting Ready for AACR 2: The Cataloger's Guide.* Librarian Series. White Plains, NY: Knowledge Industry Publications, 1980.

Hunter, Eric J. *AACR 2: An Introduction to the Second Edition of Anglo-American Cataloguing Rules.* Rev. ed. London: C. Bingley; Hamden, CT: Linnet Books, 1979.

Hunter, Eric J. *AACR 2: An Introduction to the Second Edition of the Anglo-American Cataloguing Rules* [programmed text]. Hamden, CT: Shoe String Press, 1979.

Kelm, Carol R. "The Historical Development of the Second Edition of Anglo-American Cataloguing Rules." *Library Resources and Technical Services* 22 (Winter 1978): 22-23.

The Making of a Code. Edited by Doris H. Clack. International Conference on AACR 2, Tallahassee, Florida, 1978. Chicago: American Library Association, 1978.

Malinconico, S. Michael, and Paul J. Fasana. *The Future of the Catalog: The Library's Choices.* White Plains, NY: Knowledge Industry Publications, 1979.

Massonneau, Suzanne. "Developments in the Organization of Audiovisual Materials." *Library Trends* 25 (January 1977): 665-84.

Maxwell, Margaret F. *Handbook for AACR 2: Explaining and Illustrating Anglo-American Cataloguing Rules.* Second Edition. Chicago: American Library Association, 1980.

Olson, Nancy B. *Cataloging of Audiovisual Materials: A Manual Based on AACR 2.* Mankato, MN: Minnesota Scholarly Press, 1981.

Problems in Bibliographic Access to Nonprint Materials: Project Media Base Final Report. Washington, DC: National Commission on Libraries and Information Science, 1979.

Project Media Base: A National Data Base for Audiovisual Resources. Washington, DC: National Commission on Libraries and Information Science, 1976.

Richmond, Phyllis A. "AACR 2—A Review Article." *Journal of Academic Librarianship* 6 (March 1980): 30-37.

Rogers, JoAnn V. "Cataloging Nonprint Materials in School Media Centers." *School Library Journal* (April 1978): 51-53.

Rogers, JoAnn V. "Mainstreaming Media Center Materials: Adopting AACR 2." *School Library Journal* (April 1981): 32-35.

Rogers, JoAnn V. "Nonprint Cataloging: A Call for Standardization." *American Libraries* 10 (January 1979): 46-48.

Simonton, Wesley. "An Introduction to AACR 2." *Library Resources and Technical Services* 23 (Summer 1979): 321-39.

Weihs, Jean, Shirley Lewis, and Janet MacDonald. *Nonbook Materials: The Organization of Integrated Collections.* Ottawa, ON: Canadian Library Association, 1979.

Weintraub, D. Kathryn. "AACR 2: A Review Article." *Library Quarterly* 49 (October 1979): 435-43.

Wynar, Bohdan S., Arlene Taylor Dowell, and Jeanne Osborn. *Introduction to Cataloging and Classification.* 6th Edition. Littleton, CO: Libraries Unlimited, Inc., 1980. [Part II is an introductory text to cataloging, using AACR 2.]

Yarborough, Judith D. *Access to Nonprint Media: What Is and What May Be.* Washington, DC: ERIC Clearinghouse on Information Resources, 1976. (ED 119 743).

Appendix III

Bibliography of Nonprint Bibliographies: Guides to Nonprint Bibliographies, Lists, Indexes, and Selection Tools

Bonn, Thomas L., comp. *A Guide to Audio-Visual References: Selection and Ordering Sources.* Stanford, CA: ERIC Clearinghouse on Information Resources, 1977. (ED 148 371).
Annotated list of audiovisual reference sources giving library locations. Divided by subjects, including general sources in all media formats, reviews, guides, bibliographies, media types, hardware, indexes and abstracts, and periodicals.

Carter, Yvonne, comp. *Aids to Media Selection for Students and Teachers.* Washington, DC: U.S. Government Printing Office, 1971.
Annotated bibliography describes selected book lists and periodicals which review books, audiovisual materials, and multiethnic instructional materials. Sources cited contain reviews of materials for pupils from the elementary grades through high school. However, no attempt has been made to separate the lists according to school level. A directory of publishers and an author-title index are included.

Carter, Yvonne, et al. *Supplement to Aids to Media Selection for Students and Teachers.* Washington, DC: U.S. Department of Health, Education, and Welfare, U.S. Government Printing Office, 1973.
A selected list of the book lists and periodicals published or revised since 1970 which review books, audiovisual or multiethnic instructional materials suitable for use in elementary and secondary school instructional programs. Contains 508 sources which offer bibliographic information, directory of publishers, and author-title index.

Chisholm, Margaret E. *Media Indexes and Review Sources.* College Park, MD: University of Maryland, College of Library and Information Services, 1972.
Bibliographical information and comments on more than 80 indexes and review sources for audiovisual materials. Designed to assist in making nonprint materials more accessible and to identify sources of evaluative reviews. Indexes by subject and by type of media are included.

Educational Media Yearbook. New York: R. R. Bowker Co., 1973-1979; Littleton, CO: Libraries Unlimited, Inc., 1980- .
Section entitled Mediagraphy contains classified and alphabetical lists of reference tools in the area of audiovisuals, media-related periodicals and newsletters, and media about media. Guides to organizations and associations

concerned with audiovisuals, as well as funding sources, publishers, producers, and distributors are included.

Hart, Thomas L., Mary Alice Hunt, and Blanche Woolls. *Multi-media Indexes, Lists, and Review Sources: A Bibliographic Guide.* New York: Marcel Dekker, Inc., 1975.
This book identifies and describes over 400 bibliographic tools and selection sources of both print and nonprint media which are currently available.

Limbacher, James L. *A Reference Guide to Audiovisual Information.* New York: R. R. Bowker, Co., 1972.
Annotated bibliography of books, periodicals, and reference works which are devoted to or review audiovisual materials, includes publishers' addresses and a listing of audiovisual terms and their definitions.

Mirwis, A. N. *Guides to Educational Media Software.* Brooklyn, NY: Educational Media Information Service, 1977.
Subject guide to bibliographies, lists, catalogs, monographs, and other selection aids for audiovisual materials. Volume is divided by broad subject categories such as geography, history, mathematics, nutrition, etc. and includes a title and keyword index.

Moses, Kathlyn J., comp. *Aids to Media Selection for Students and Teachers.* Washington, DC: U.S. Department of Health, Education, and Welfare, 1976.
Update of the 1971 edition is a selected list of bibliographies and journals which review books, periodicals, and audiovisual materials. Only reviewing tools published since 1970 are included. Sources cited contain reviews of materials for pupils from the elementary grades through high school; however, no attempt has been made to separate the lists according to school level. A directory of publishers and an author-title index are included.

Newsome, Walter. *New Guide to Popular Government Publications: For Libraries and Home Reference.* Littleton, CO: Libraries Unlimited, Inc., 1978.
2,500 new or favorite documents for popular use are described with explanations of where and how to obtain print and audiovisual materials.

Perkins, Flossie. *Book and Non-book Media: Annotated Guide to Selection Aids for Educational Materials.* Urbana, IL: National Council of Teachers of English, 1972.
Alphabetical list of selection aids for audiovisual educational materials. Detailed annotations include bibliographic and subject information, evaluation, scope, and references to similar tools. Indexes arranged according to intended audience, title, and author/publisher. Useful aid for school librarians and public librarians.

Rogers, A. Robert. *The Humanities: A Selective Guide to Information Sources.* 2nd ed. Littleton, CO: Libraries Unlimited, Inc., 1979.
Rogers' book serves as both a textbook and as a guide to information sources in the humanities.

Rufsvold, Margaret I., and Carolyn Guss. *Guides to Educational Media.* 3rd ed. Chicago: American Library Association, 1971.
This comprehensive guide identifies and provides descriptive annotations for 153 media catalogs and indexes. Each entry provides bibliographic information as well as information on scope, arrangement, entries, and special features. A list of 36 specialized periodicals which systematically provide information on nonprint educational media is also included.

Rufsvold, Margaret Irene. *Guides to Educational Media: Films, Filmstrips, Multimedia Kits, Programmed Instruction Materials, Recordings on Discs and Tapes, Slides, Transparencies, Videotapes.* 4th ed. Chicago: American Library Association, 1977.
245 educational media catalogs, indexes, and reviewing services are described. In addition, 35 related publications are mentioned in the annotations.

Sive, Mary Robinson. *Selecting Instructional Media: A Guide to Audiovisual and Other Instructional Media Lists.* Littleton, CO: Libraries Unlimited, Inc., 1978.
Annotated bibliography of audiovisual guides, monographs, periodicals, and catalogs arranged by subject and media format. Includes comprehensive media lists and numerous indexes.

Woodbury, Marda. *Selecting Materials for Instruction: Issues and Policies.* Littleton, CO: Libraries Unlimited, Inc., 1979.
Covers issues relating to selection of instructional media materials from pre-school through secondary level. Author offers background discussion, selection criteria, charts, and extensive references and recommended reading in the area of audiovisual media selection. Format information is generally included throughout the text. Strength is in bibliographic references.

Wynar, Christine L. *Guide to Reference Books for School Media Centers.* Littleton, CO: Libraries Unlimited, Inc., 1973.
Contains 2,575 annotated entries for reference books and selection tools for use in elementary, junior, and senior high schools. Some tools include nonprint.

Wynar, Christine L. *1974-75 Supplement: Guide to Reference Books for School Media Centers.* Littleton, CO: Libraries Unlimited, Inc., 1976.
Supplement adds 518 titles to the *Guide to Reference Books for School Media Centers.* Some tools include nonprint.

Wynar, Christine G. *Guide to Reference Books for School Media Centers.* 2nd ed. Littleton, CO: Libraries Unlimited, Inc., 1981.
New edition of standard titles with some tools which include nonprint.

Appendix IV
Selected Titles Explaining Nonprint Formats

American Geographical Society. *Cataloging and Filing Rules for Maps and Atlases in the Society's Collections.* New York: American Geographical Society, 1969.

Ballard, John R., and Calvin E. Mether. *Audio-visual Fundamentals: Basic Equipment Operations and Simple Materials Production.* 2nd ed. Dubuque, IA: Wm. C. Brown Co., 1979.
Provides self-instruction in operation of basic audiovisual equipment and production of simple instructional materials. Step-by-step instructions. Illustrated.

Bensinger, Charles. *The Video Guide.* Santa Barbara, CA: Video-Info Publications, 1980.
While the focus of this text is primarily video hardware, chapter six concerns the videotape itself—a comparison of videotape and film, a description of the types of videotape and how it works, and information on the care of these materials.

Bergen, John V. "Map Reading and Map Appreciation," *Illinois Libraries* 56 (May 1974): 349-59.

Brodatz, Phil. *Photo GRAPHIC Techniques.* Rochester, NY: Eastman Kodak Co., 1979.
General introduction to graphic arts materials and techniques which utilize photography.

Cabeceiras, James. *The Multimedia Library.* New York: Academic Press, 1978.
Examines the various media found in libraries with an emphasis on identification and application. Separate chapters are devoted to microforms, 16mm and 8mm films, filmstrips, slides, audio recordings, television, and three-dimensional objects. Each chapter includes its own bibliography. Text includes numerous illustrations, photographs, and comparison charts.

Caranicas, Peter, ed. *The Video Handbook.* 3rd ed. New York: United Business Publications, Inc., 1977.
A guide to setting up and running a video system. Articles by leading system managers, technical consultants, and video production personnel offer step-by-step guidance from initial purchase of video equipment to advanced video production. Many charts and tables with data on equipment and services are included.

Diaz, Albert James, ed. *Microforms in Libraries.* Weston, CT: Microform Review, Inc., 1975.
Collection of articles on microforms with discussion and comparison of microfilm, microfiche, aperture cards, and microopaques. Information on selection, cataloging, storage, and standards are included.

Dove, Jack. *The Audio Visual.* London: Andre Deutsch, Ltd., 1975.
Explanations of the various media formats, complete with a historical background on each form. Text includes guidelines for selection, standards, classification, cataloging, storage, and preservation. There is also a brief discussion of audiovisual equipment and a purchasing directory.

Dranov, Paula. *Microfilm: The Librarians' View, 1976-77.* White Plains, NY: Knowledge Industry Publications, Inc., 1976.
An overview of library microforms including specific information on the various formats and their use. Much of the information in this volume is in tabular form. Includes bibliography.

Fothergill, Richard, and Ian Burchart. *Non-Book Materials in Libraries.* Hamden, CT: Linnet Books, 1978.
This well-organized and comprehensive text is divided into five principle sections: history and terminology, the user, the materials, the user and the materials, and management of an audiovisual center. The materials chapter explores the various formats and includes many illustrations, tables, and charts. The "user and the materials" chapter examines each format from the acquisitions, cataloging, storage, and retrieval aspects. Includes references, bibliography, and comprehensive index.

Gaddy, Dale. *A Microform Handbook.* Silver Spring, MD: National Microfilm Association, 1974.
Primer for persons unfamiliar with uses of microfilm. Defines basic terminology, reviews micrographics field, and focuses upon the different types of microforms and their selection. Includes many diagrams and charts.

Goudket, Michael. *An Audiovisual Primer.* New York: Teachers College Press, 1973.
General introduction to films, audiotapes, videotapes, and graphic materials. Includes their use in the classroom, simple equipment repair, and sources of supplies and further information. Contains many illustrations and individual glossaries at the end of each chapter.

Hardwood, Don. *Everything You Always Wanted to Know about Portable Videotape Recordings.* 3rd ed. Soyosset, NY: VTR Publishing Co., 1978.
A basic video handbook, ideal for beginners. Includes many photographs and illustrations.

Irvine, Betty Jo, and Eileen Fry. *Slide Libraries: A Guide for Academic Institutions, Museums, and Special Collections.* Littleton, CO: Libraries Unlimited, Inc., 1979.
Manual on slide librarianship which includes classification and cataloging, organization, storage, bibliographies, and a directory of manufacturers and distributors.

Isaacs, Dan Lee, and Robert Glen George. *Instructional Media: Selection and Utilization.* Dubuque, IA: Kendall/Hunt Publishing Co., 1971.
Contains chapters on graphics, filmstrips, slides, transparencies, audio recordings, videotapes, and 16mm film. Discusses the characteristics as well as the strengths and weaknesses of each format. There are suggestions for utilization within the classroom and an appendix which includes a bibliography of basic, instructional media texts and a glossary of terms.

Kemp, Jerrold E. *Planning and Producing Audio Visual Materials.* 3rd ed. New York: Thomas Y. Crowell, Inc., 1975.
Includes separate chapters on each media format as well as detailed instructions on producing audiovisual materials. The text contains many illustrations and is organized around a systematic approach which carries the user from the organization of a concept through to a professionally produced audiovisual product. Comparison charts and a subject bibliography are included.

Kenney, Brigitte L., and Roberto Esteves. *Video and Cable Communications: Guidelines for Librarians.* Chicago: American Library Association, Information Science and Automation Division, 1975.
Videotape packaging (reel-to-reel, cartridge, cassette, videodisc), dimensions, and standards are discussed in this handbook. It is designed primarily to explore the potential uses of video and cable technologies in extending traditional library services.

Langford, M. J. *Visual Aids and Photography in Education.* New York: Focal Press, Inc., Hastings House Publishers, n.d.
Practical manual on production of educationally sound visual aids by the working teacher or instructor. Offers "how to" directions and compares the possibilities and limitations of different types of media.

Laird, Dugan. *A User's Look at the Audio-Visual World.* 2nd ed. Fairfax, VA: National Audio-Visual Association, Inc., 1974.
Brief, simple text discusses each media format, its advantages, disadvantages, and necessary equipment for use. Includes a section on standardization of audiovisual materials and equipment. Much of text written in outline form with comparison charts and checklists. Includes bibliography.

Laubacher, Marilyn R. *Brief Resource Guide to Sources of Information about Microform Equipment.* Stanford, CA: ERIC Clearinghouse on Resources, 1979.
Annotations of books, directories and guides, and articles concerning micropublications.

Minor, Edward O. *Handbook for Preparing Visual Media.* New York: McGraw Hill, Inc., 1978.
Teaches professional techniques of visual media design and production. Simple step-by-step approach includes hundreds of illustrations, quick-check selection charts, and annotated bibliography.

National Center for Education Statistics. *Educational Technology: A Handbook of Standard Terminology and a Guide for Recording and Reporting Information about Educational Technology.* Washington, DC: U.S. Department of Health, Education, and Welfare, 1975. (State Educational Records and Reports Series: Handbook X).
Provides a standard list of media terms with definitions and suggested units of measure. This publication helps to ensure compatible recording and reporting of audiovisual data.

Overman, Michael. *Understanding Sound, Video, and Film Recording.* Blue Ridge Summit, PA: TAB Books, 1978.
History and present-day developments in the field of audio and video recording.

Quinly, William J. *The Selection, Acquisition, & Utilization of Audiovisual Materials.* 2nd ed. Pullman, WA: Information Futures, 1978.
Comprehensive coverage of media software, includes information on motion pictures, slides, transparencies, sound recordings, microforms, videotapes, and related media procedures, such as photography, dry mounting, equipment acquisition, and information networking. Each chapter includes a discussion of types and sizes within a particular format, care, storage, utilization, advantages and disadvantages, and special use recommendations.

Robinson, J. F. *Using Videotape.* New York: Focal Press, Inc., Hastings House Publishers, 1976.
Basic guide for all videotape recorder users. Explains how to get the best results from each machine and its accessories in simple terms.

Robinson, J. F. *Videotape Recording: Theory and Practice.* New York: Hastings House Publishers, Focal Press, Inc., 1979.
Provides comprehensive coverage of the whole field for both students and professionals. Describes videotape recording equipment in current use, closed circuit systems, material on cassettes, cartridges, etc.

Robinson, Richard. *The Video Primer.* New York: Links Books Publishers, 1974.
Guide to ½-inch videocassette equipment, production, and concepts. Also includes information on software.

Romiszowski, A. J. *The Selection and Use of Instructional Media.* New York: John Wiley and Sons, Inc., 1974.
Formats divided according to still or sound media, or combinations of both. Includes detailed sections on television, simulations, and games. Few illustrations. References with each chapter.

Selecting Media for Learning: Readings from Audiovisual Instruction. Washington, DC: Association for Educational Communications and Technology, 1974.
This book contains 31 articles reprinted from *Audiovisual Instruction*, some of which discuss and evaluate various formats for audiovisual materials. Many articles include bibliographies.

Teague, S. J. *Microform Librarianship.* London: Boston, Butterworth & Co., Ltd., 1977.
Outlines the various microformats—card, film, and fiche—offering their dimensions, availability, strengths and weaknesses, uses, and necessary equipment. Includes illustrations and references.

Veaner, Allen B. *The Evaluation of Micropublications: A Handbook for Librarians.* Chicago: American Library Association, 1971.
Complete guide to microforms. Includes information on various formats, film size, stock and coatings, image legibility, and archival permanence. No illustrations. Classified bibliography includes both monographs and journal articles.

Wittich, Walter Arno, and Charles Francis Schuller. *Audiovisual Materials: Their Nature and Use.* 4th ed. New York: Harper and Row, 1967.
This media textbook, geared toward the elementary classroom teacher, treats each format separately. There are especially good sections on the making and use of graphics including diagrams, charts, posters, photos, and pictures. There is also a detailed discussion of maps and globes, excluded from many other texts of this kind. Many illustrations. Chapter summaries.

Wittich, Walter A., and Charles F. Schuller. *Instructional Technology: Its Nature and Use.* New York: Harper and Row, 1979.
A basic text for use in college and university courses in audiovisual education. Includes theoretical and practical considerations for three-dimensional teaching materials, community study, displays, audio materials, still projection, motion pictures, simulations, and games.

Woodbury, Marda. *Selecting Materials for Instruction: Media and the Curriculum.* Littleton, CO: Libraries Unlimited, Inc., 1979.
Handbook for elementary and secondary school educators on the selection of print and nonprint formats, including films, games, and photographs.

Wyman, Raymond. *Mediaware: Selection, Operation and Maintenance.* 2nd ed. Dubuque, IA: Wm. C. Brown Co., 1976.
While this text is devoted primarily to media hardware, it does contain a great deal of good information concerning the selection and characteristics of slides, films, transparencies, sound recordings, and videotape. Illustrations, charts, and tables complement the written descriptions. The book includes detailed information on sizes, dimensions, and recording speeds, and also describes the process by which many of these formats are made.

Yeamans, George T. *Mounting and Preserving Pictorial Materials: A Programmed Primer.* Muncie, IN: Ball State University, 1976.
Pictures, maps, charts, and photographs are the focus of this self-instructional workbook, which offers instructions on mounting, framing, and preserving pictorial materials. Drawings and diagrams are used to help teach basic techniques.

Yeamans, George T. *Tape Recording Made Easy: A Programmed Primer.* Muncie, IN: Ball State University, 1978.

This workbook, designed to give the basic principles and terminology involved in the operation of reel-to-reel and cassette tape recorders, includes information on audio software, size, construction, and varieties as well as useful data on recording speeds, tracking, measurements, etc.

Yeamans, George T. *Transparency Making Made Easy.* Muncie, IN: Ball State University, 1977.
A workbook which offers simple instructions for making inexpensive visuals for use with an overhead projector. Several techniques are discussed and compared with many supporting illustrations.

Yeamans, George T. *Projectionists' Programmed Primer.* Muncie, IN: Ball State University, 1975.
This self-instructional workbook teaches the basic principles and terminology involved in handling transparencies, slides, filmstrips, motion pictures, and their projection equipment. Drawings and diagrams are an integral part of the text. Appendices include a glossary and checklists to help determine causes of software damage and equipment malfunctions.

Appendix V
Selected Bibliographies, Directories, and Indexes: Sources of Nonprint Bibliographic Information

Aceto, Vincent J., Jane Graves, and Fred Silva, eds. *Film Literature Index.* Albany, NY: State University of New York at Albany; Filmdex, 1973- . (Annual).

American Library Association, Audio Visual Committee. *Films for Libraries Selected by a Subcommittee of the American Library Association, Audio-Visual Committee.* Chicago: American Library Association, 1962.

American Film Institute. *Catalog of Holdings: American Film Institute and United Artists Collection.* Beverly Hills, CA: The Institute, n.d.

Armitage, Andrew D., and Dean Tudor. *Annual Index to Popular Music Record Reviews.* Metuchen, NJ: Scarecrow Press, 1975. (Annual).

Aros, Andrew A., ed. *A Title Guide to the Talkies, 1964 through 1974.* Metuchen, NJ: Scarecrow Press, 1977.

Audio Cassette Directory. Glendale, CA: Cassette Information Services, n.d.

Audio-text Cassettes—Reference Catalog. North Hollywood, CA: Center for Cassette Studies, 1975.

Baer, D. Richard, ed. *Film Buff's Checklist of Motion Pictures (1912-1979).* Hollywood, CA: Hollywood Film Archive, [1980].

Batty, Linda. *Retrospective Index to Film Periodicals, 1930-1971.* New York: R. R. Bowker Co., 1975.

Bell, Irene Wood, and Jeanne E. Wieckert. *Basic Media Skills through Games.* Littleton, CO: Libraries Unlimited, Inc., 1979.

Bell, Irene Wood, and Jeanne E. Wieckert. *Basic Classroom Skills through Games.* Littleton, CO: Libraries Unlimited, Inc., 1979.

Billboard International Buyer's Guide. Los Angeles, CA: Billboard Publications, Inc., 1948- . (Annual).

Bowker, Karen Jones. *International Index to Film Periodicals, 1973-1974.* New York: St. Martin's Press, 1975- .

Bowles, Stephen F., ed. *Index to Critical Film Reviews in British and American Film Periodicals together with Index to Critical Reviews about Film.* New York: Burt Franklin and Co., Inc., 1974.

Brooks, Tim, and Earle Marsh, comps. *The Complete Directory to Prime Time Network T.V. Shows: 1946-Present.* New York: Ballantine Books, 1979.

Brown, Lucy Gregor. *Core Media Collection for Secondary Schools.* 2nd ed. New York: R. R. Bowker Co., 1979.

Cantwell, Zita M., and Hortense A. Doyle. *Instructional Technology: An Annotated Bibliography.* Metuchen, NJ: Scarecrow Press, 1974.

Catalog of Captioned Films for the Deaf (Educational Films). Vol. 1. Washington, DC: U.S. Department of Health, Education, and Welfare, 1974.

Catalog of United States Government Produced Audiovisual Materials. Washington, DC: General Service Administration National Archives and Records Service, National Audiovisual Center. (Annual).

Chicorel, Marietta. *Chicorel Index to Video Tapes.* Oxford, IN: American Publishing Co., 1978.

Cowie, Peter. *International Film Guide.* London: Thomas Yoseloff, Ltd., Tantivy Press. (Annual).

Dimmitt, Richard B., ed. *An Actor Guide to the Talkies: A Comprehensive Listing of 8,000 Feature-length Films from January, 1949 until December, 1964.* Metuchen, NJ: Scarecrow Press, 1967.

Education Film Library Association (EFLA) Evaluations. New York: Education Film Library Association. (Annual).

Educational Film Locator of the Consortium of University Film Centers and R. R. Bowker Company. New York: R. R. Bowker Co., 1979.

Educational Media Council of New York. *Educational Media Index.* 14 vols. New York, McGraw-Hill, 1964. Supplements, 1965.

Educators Progress Services Guides. Randolph, WI: Educator's Progress Service, rev. annually.

Educator's:

Guide to Free Audio and Video Materials. 27th ed., 1980.

Guide to Free Films. 40th ed., 1980.

Guide to Free Filmstrips. 32nd ed., 1980.

Guide to Free Guidance Materials. 19th ed., 1980.

Guide to Free Health, Physical Education and Recreation Materials. 13th ed., 1980.

Guide to Free Science Materials. 21st ed., 1980.

Guide to Free Social Studies Materials. 20th ed., 1980.

Guide to Free Tapes, Scripts, Transparencies. 26th ed., 1980.

Elementary Teachers Guide to Free Curriculum Materials. 37th ed., 1980.

Edielberg, Lawrence, ed. *Health Sciences Video Directory.* New York: Shelter Books, 1977.

Emmens, Carol A. *Short Stories on Film.* Littleton, CO: Libraries Unlimited, Inc., 1978.

The Film Daily Year Book. New York: J. W. Alicoate, 1927- .

Film Review Index. Pasadena, CA: Audio-Visual Associates, 1970-1972. (Annual). Succeeded by *International Index to Multi-Media Information.*

Gerlach, John C., and Lana Gerlach, eds. *The Critical Index: A Bibliography of Articles on Film in English, 1940-1973.* New York: Teacher's College Press, 1974.

Index to Record Reviews in Music Library Association Notes. Ann Arbor, MI: Music Library Association, 1948- . (Quarterly).

International Index to Multi-Media Information. Pasadena, CA: Audio-Visual Associates, Inc., 1970- . (Quarterly). Formerly *Film Review Index.*

International Television Almanac. New York: Quigley Publishing Co., 1956- .

Jacobs, Arthur. *The Music Yearbook.* New York: St. Martin's Press, 1973.

Landers Film Reviews. Los Angeles, CA: Landers Associates, 1956- . (5 issues per year).

The Last Whole Film Catalog. Wilmette, IL: Films, Inc., 1976.

Learning Directory 1970-71. New York: Westinghouse Learning Press, 1970. Supplement 1972-73.

Library of Congress Catalog: Motion Pictures and Filmstrips. Washington, DC: Library of Congress, Card Division, 1953- . (Quarterly with Annual and Quintennial Cumulations).

Library of Congress Catalog: Music and Phonorecords. Washington, DC: Library of Congress, Card Division, 1953- . (Semiannual with Annual cumulations).

Limbacher, James, ed. *Feature Films on 8 mm. and 16 mm.* 6th ed. New York: R. R. Bowker Co., 1979.

Listening Post. Williamsport, PA: Bro-Dart, 1969-76.

MacCann, Richard Dyer, and Edward S. Perry, eds. *The New Film Index: A Bibliography of Magazine Articles in English, 1930-1970.* New York: Dutton, 1975.

Maleady, Antoinette O. *Index to Record and Tape Reviews. A Classical Music Buying Guide 1978.* San Anselmo, CA: Chulainn Press, 1979.

Maleady, Antoinette O., comp. *Record and Tape Reviews Index.* Metuchen, NJ: Scarecrow Press, 1972- . (Annual).

Media Review Digest. Ann Arbor, MI: Pierian Press, 1973- . (Annual in two parts). Formerly *Multi-Media Reviews Index.*

Media Review: Professional Evaluations of Instructional Materials. Pleasantville, NY: 1979- . (10 issues per year, looseleaf format).

Multi-Media Review Index. Ann Arbor, MI: Pierian Press, 1970-1972.

National Audiovisual Center. *A Reference List of Audiovisual Materials Produced by the United States Government.* Washington, DC: National Audiovisual Center, 1978.

National Information Center for Educational Media. *Index to Producers and Distributors.* 5th ed. Los Angeles, CA: University of Southern California, 1980.

National Information Center for Educational Media (NICEM). *Index to Nonprint Special Education Materials—Multimedia.* Los Angeles, CA: NICEM, 1980. (Learner Volume).

National Information Center for Educational Media. *Index to Nonprint Special Education Materials—Multimedia.* Los Angeles, CA: NICEM, 1980. (Professional Volume).

National Information Center for Educational Media. *NICEM Media Indexes.* Los Angeles, CA: University of Southern California, (Periodic updates).

Index to:

Educational Audio Tapes. 5th ed., 1980.

Educational Overhead Transparencies. 6th ed., 1980.

Educational Records. 5th ed., 1980.

Educational Slides. 4th ed., 1980.

Educational Video Tapes. 5th ed., 1980.

8 mm. Motion Cartridges. 6th ed., 1980.

16 mm. Educational Films. 7th ed., 1980.

35 mm. Filmstrips. 7th ed., 1980.

National Library of Medicine AVLINE Catalog. Bethesda, MD: National Library of Medicine. (Annual).

National Park Service Film Collection. Washington, DC: National Audio Visual Center, National Archives Trust Fund Board, 1979.

North American Film and Video Directory. New York: R. R. Bowker Co., 1976.

Parish, James. *Astor's Television Credits 1950-1972.* Metuchen, NJ: Scarecrow Press, 1973.

Pavlakis, Christopher. *The American Music Handbook.* New York: Free Press, 1974.

Phonolog. Los Angeles, CA: Trade Service Publications, 1948- . (Weekly).

A Reference List of Audio Visual Materials Produced by the U.S. Government. Fairfax, VA: National Audio Visual Center, 1978.

Sandberg, Larry, and Dick Weissman. *The Folk Music Sourcebook.* New York: Alfred A. Knopf, Inc., 1976.

Schwann-1 Record and Tape Guide. Boston, MA: A B C Schwann Publications, Inc., 1949- . (Monthly).

Schwann-2 Record and Tape Guide. Boston, MA: A B C Schwann Publications, Inc., 1949- . (Supplement to monthly Schwann-1).

SOURCES: 1979: A Guide to Print and Nonprint Materials. Syracuse, NY: Gaylord Brothers, Inc., 1979.

Sprecher, Daniel, comp. *Guide to Government Loan Films.* 3rd ed. Alexandria, VA: Serina Press, 1974.

Terrace, Vincent. *The Complete Encyclopedia of Television Programs 1947-1976.* New York: A. S. Barnes and Co., 1976.

Union List of Audiovisuals in the Library Network. Washington, DC: Veterans Administration, 1976.

Van Orden, Phyllis, ed. *The Elementary School Library Collection: A Guide to Books and Other Media, Phases 1-2-3.* 10th ed. New Brunswick, NJ: Bro-Dart Foundation, 1976.

Video Program Catalog. Washington, DC: The Public Television Library, Department of the Public Broadcasting Service, 1976-1977.

The Video Programs Index. Syosset, NY: The National Video Clearinghouse, Inc., 1979.

The Video Register: 1979-1980. White Plains, NY: Knowledge Industry Publications, 1979.

The Video Source Book. 2nd ed. Syosset, NY: The National Video Clearinghouse, Inc., 1979.

The Videolog: Programs for General Interest and Entertainment, 1979. New York: Esselte Video, Inc., 1979.

Weaver, John T., comp. *Forty Years of Screen Credits 1929-1969.* Metuchen, NJ: Scarecrow Press, 1970.

Winslow, Ken. *Video Source Book.* Syosset, NY: National Video Clearinghouse, 1979.

Winslow, Ken, ed. *Video Programs Index.* Syosset, NY: National Video Clearinghouse, 1979.

Index

ALA, 24
Access points, 165-70
  sources of information, 165-66
Accompanying material
  cartographic materials, 61
    notes on, 62
  graphic materials, 120-22
    as source of information, 114
    notes on, 126
    recorded in physical description area,
      120-21
  motion pictures and videorecordings
    notes on, 103
    recorded in physical description area, 53-54
  sound recordings
    notes on, 82
  three-dimensional artefacts and realia, 145-46
    notes on, 147
Adaptations of art works
  entry, 168
Added entries, 169-70
  collaborators, 169
  corporate bodies, 170
  related works, 170
  writers, 169
Alternative formats, notes on
  graphic materials, 126-27
  microforms, 161
  motion pictures and videorecordings, 104
  sound recordings, 83
American Library Association, 24
Anglo-American Cataloguing Committee for
  Cartographic Materials, 57
Areas of description, 36-37
  see also Title and statement of responsibility
  area; Edition area; Material (or type of publication); specific area; Publication, distribution, etc., area; Physical description area;
  Series area; Note area; Standard number and
  terms of availability area.
Art originals
  date, 117
  definition, 43
  for other rules see Graphic materials
Art works, adaptations of
  entry, 168
Audience of item, notes on
  graphic materials, 126
  sound recordings, 82-83
  three-dimensional artefacts and realia, 147-48

Audiovisual Market Place, 18-19
Availability, terms of, notes on
  see Terms of availability
AVLINE, 19-20

Bibliographic control
  local cataloging guidelines, 26-27
  prior to AACR 2, 24-28
  standardization, 15-18

Cartographic materials, 57-65
  collections, 59
  definition, 46, 57
  edition area, 60
  in microform, 159
  levels of description, 58
  mathematical data area, 60
  multilevel description, 59
  note area, 61-62
  physical description area, 60-61
  projection, 60
  publication, distribution, etc., area, 60
  scale, 60
  sources of information, 58
  title and statement of responsibility area,
    59-60
Cartridges, film, 95
Cartridges, sound
  see Sound cartridges
Cassettes, film, 95-96
Cassettes, sound
  see Sound cassettes
Cast
  see Performers, notes on
Celestial globes
  for rules see Cartographic materials
Certification requirements, 20-21
Charts
  definition, 43
  for other rules see Graphic materials; Cartographic materials
Chief source of information
  see Sources of information
Collaborators
  added entries, 169
Collation
  see Physical description area